The Kingdom of Creators

A Christian Worldview for the Coming Millennia

By: Clarity

Table of Contents

Introduction

The Kingdom of Creators is designed for those who intend to lead themselves, the church, and all humanity toward fulfilling the Great Imperative of human existence, that of orchestrating a world of unique worlds. Such individuals must first adopt the creator's perspective, enabling them to rule from the spiritual realm in a way that will fill their inner realm with the means to uniquely subdue their personal portion of the material realm. Only then may such world-making sovereigns begin to embrace the doctrines needed to interconnect humanity's lost past with our perplexing present as a means to illuminate a path toward our shared future. Finally, those who are living as the Kingdom of Creators will work together toward keeping everyone from getting into a position of authority over anyone—especially themselves—to ensure each one might make the world that only they can make so that humanity might return to being a race of unique world makers who are making Mother Nature into a world of unique worlds, for the World Maker.

Part 1
A Creator's Perspective

As fallen beings, it's disconcerting to reorient our perspective toward being a creator since doing so reminds us far too much of what we've lost. Still, doing so is necessary if nothing more than to allow us a reasonable level of survivability, comfort, and orchestration with other human beings. Moreover, the potential for partnership with creation also relies exclusively upon our ability to present ourselves as spiritual beings capable of artistically orchestrating her material treasures. However, the ultimate aim in altering the way we perceive ourselves is to reclaim a small portion of what we lost so long ago, that of being creators who walk with the Creator.

Section 1
Partnering with Creators

Although human beings are the least significant partners in the orchestration of our unique world, partnering with other sovereign souls remains a vital skill for any world-making creator. We successfully partner with other world makers by first considering what we all value, thereby allowing us to produce accordingly and make ourselves indispensable to all. Then, we'll need to discern exactly what everyone around us is trying to achieve so we might make our world in a way that assists others toward making their world so that we all might work together toward bringing forth a world of unique worlds. Lastly, we must exercise a realistic judgment regarding which souls are safe to bring close to our world-making effort and which to keep at arm's length.

Chapter 1
What We Value

All human interactions have been, remain, and will continue to be contentious. Any attempt to change or ignore this fundamental truth will always end catastrophically. The failure inherent to every past effort toward building a utopian dream stands as an indelible warning against any such future foolishness. Human beings do not live together in peace, harmony, and boundless love. Human beings exist together in a perpetual state of contention. Only after we embrace this reality may we realistically form the partnerships necessary to orchestrate a world of unique worlds.

Fortunately, a workaround to humanity's contentious nature already exists. In fact, each of us exercises this art regularly. There is a reason we do not remove that one unbearable extended family member from the plane of human existence. Whether we acknowledge it or not, allowing them to live provides us with something valuable. Perhaps they bake a wicked apple pie, or they care for animals in a way that diverts our smoldering wrath. However, it is more likely that unleashing our righteous judgment upon them would inadvertently hurt someone else in the family that we deeply love. Therefore, the workaround to the contentious nature of human interaction is to understand and then offer to one another what we all recognize as valuable.

Human beings recognize value in three sequential tiers: survival, comfort, and orchestration. If we help someone survive comfortably—in a way that expands and enriches their efforts toward orchestrating their unique world—then they'll recognize us as an indispensable partner. Likewise, if they help us survive comfortably in a way that expands and enriches our orchestrational efforts, then the foundation for a mutually beneficial partnership is laid.

Survival is the foremost human value. If we don't have enough food to eat, sufficient shelter to ward off frostbite, or if our neighbors are warmongering cannibals, then we could care less about life's comforts or the means to orchestrate our own unique world. Survival is always the foundation of human existence. And so, when attempting to interact with others, our first forward step must always be to create a mutually beneficial assurance of survival. Only after we're confident in the goodwill of others in enabling us to survive will we consider reaching together toward everyone's comfort and everyone's orchestration.

Not only are individuals motivated by humanity's three sequential values, but so is our entire species. If we consider the first five millennia of recorded human history, we'll see mankind utterly fixated on survival. While surrounded by enemies itching for ethnic cleansing and having a food production system that would often fail after a month of inclement weather, no one could easily extend their reach beyond the day-to-day struggle for survival. Only the richest one percent of the top one percent, namely kings and lords, even sampled the few comforts available. Such privileged individuals also dabbled haphazardly in world-making, which usually resulted in the warfare that regularly threatened the survival of all.

Not until around the dawn of the Roman Empire did a significant percentage of any one civilization start experiencing a reasonable level of survival alongside many basic creature comforts. During this first larger-scale transition to the second tier of human value, it's important to note that Roman society also experienced a notable surge in creativity. Whenever large numbers of human beings establish a reasonable level of survival and comfort together, they inevitably begin reaching toward orchestrating their world alongside everyone else's world so that humanity might bring forth a world of unique worlds.

After the fall of the Roman Empire, many cultures slipped back into the daily struggle for survival. More than a millennium passed as humanity tried to stabilize the first tier of human value. Finally, we appear to have reached a turning point with the Enlightenment. The foundation of the Enlightenment lay in a population that was reasonably affirmed in its continuing survival alongside expanding access to many creature comforts. As is always the case when this happens, those living a comfortable survival started turning their efforts toward ensuring the orchestration of their own unique world. Consequently, the Enlightenment rightly concluded that the best way to ensure one's personal freedom in orchestrating a unique world was to ensure the personal freedom of everyone in orchestrating a unique world.

Since the Enlightenment, humanity's access to a life of comfortable survival has continued to expand. Despite regular setbacks due to things like wars, famines, and natural disasters, a larger and larger percentage of human beings have begun experiencing a life of comfortable survival. As a species, it seems we've finally gotten a taste of the possibilities inherent within the final tier of human value.

The Industrial Revolution, coupled with an explosion in agricultural productivity, has now placed the food of survival and appliances of comfort into unparalleled circulation. Humanity's increasing access to a life of comfortable survival has now allowed a previously unthinkable percentage of human beings to start reaching toward making their unique world. Despite our continuing inability to ensure the comfortable survival of every human being, our species has never been so ideally positioned to begin a mass movement toward the final tier of human value.

Bringing these three values back into our personal perspective will illuminate how we might make ourselves into ideal partners for others. First, we should strive to ensure the survival of everyone around us. For example, not routinely threatening our neighbors with physical dismemberment goes a long way toward portraying ourselves as desirable

13

partners. Still, merely promising not to decapitate others in their sleep and steal all their possessions is a tepid assurance amidst the contentious nature of human interaction.

As aspiring creators, we may go further in being valuable to everyone's survival by willfully submitting to an impartial legal authority that, despite glaring imperfections, will try to ensure that everyone survives. Although such a view of government is a bit idealized, the alternative is to entrust our survival to anarchy or a dictator, of which neither holds an impressive track record for cultivating anyone's survival, comfort, or orchestration.

The fact that we willfully consent to governmental oversight reveals how deeply we fear the contentious nature of human interaction. Ensuring our survival by giving unassailable military power to a single governmental institution seems insane, particularly amidst the warfare that governments regularly engage in, which has resulted in some of the greatest horrors ever endured by mankind. Even though governmental institutions have often been the perpetrator of incalculable death and countless decades of horrifying discomfort, we still choose them over anarchy and dictators because direct human oversight is always far worse.

The best way to ensure our personal survival in the present age is to build and submit ourselves to a system designed to ensure everyone's survival. For that reason, if the governmental system works to ensure that all survive, there's a reasonable chance that we, as individuals, will receive the same benefit. Still, governmental systems remain flawed due to each being created by and run by flawed human beings. Although a shared governmental system is not a perfect solution to ensure our survival, it currently remains the best option.

By not regularly threatening our neighbors with violence and willfully submitting ourselves to a shared governmental system, we go a long way to ensure the survival of our neighbors and ourselves. Next, we

14

must consider how to also offer comfort to our fellow human beings. For example, not blasting music from our windows at two in the morning will provide a tangible level of comfort to the sleep cycle of our neighbors. Additionally, being generally pleasant during conversations—although not natural amidst the contentious nature of mankind—will help each individual we interact with experience a more comfortable life. Although these are overly simplistic examples, if we seek to develop partnerships with other human beings, we must find ways to display our goodwill regarding both their survival and their comfort.

We risk the dangers inherent to partnering with other human creators because we're finite. Since none of us is the all-powerful, all-knowing, and all-present One, we'll likely require some assistance in orchestrating the vast, complex world we intend. If we want those partners, then we must find ways to deliver not only survival and comfort to others but also the means to assist them as they orchestrate their own unique world alongside our unique world within God's world of unique worlds.

Providing our neighbors with the means to survive comfortably is far easier than providing them with orchestrational value. As human beings, we each perceive ourselves as working on something important, something undisclosed, and something only we can accomplish. The problem is we only have a vague idea of what that is.

As a species, we've fallen so far from our Creator's original design that it's difficult for us to even consider ourselves as world makers. The unfathomable mastery displayed by the World Maker during the first seven days so shames our pitiful attempts at orchestration that we find it preferable to remain ignorant of our creative likeness. Still, the desire to create our own unique world burns within every soul, impelling each to strive toward a comfortable survival so they might reach toward establishing their own unique world within God's world.

One difficulty we'll find when striving toward forming orchestrational partnerships with other human beings is that few even understand that our species is designed for world-making. For example, gambling and lotteries ensnare significant percentages of the human population because they subtly promise the means for world-making success. To a soul utterly ignorant of how to create their own unique world, a boatload of money seems like the solution. After all, having the liquefied means to summon forth whatever one desires seems like the secret to creating a unique world. Unfortunately, as the tragic stories surrounding those who've experienced a financial windfall warn us, having the means to create does not make one a creator.

Another difficulty we face in providing orchestrational value to our fellow human beings is that each soul—and, by extension, the world they're attempting to create—is unique. Therefore, the orchestrational value we offer to others must be customized to each creator and the world they're striving to bring forth. Even worse, most souls remain utterly ignorant of their creative intentions, causing them to remain fixated on the first two tiers of human value, leaving orchestration as a distant possibility but not a present reality.

Orchestrating a unique world remains a fantasy for most of our fellow human beings, making the provision of customized orchestrational value for the world that they're not even making rather problematic. However, humanity's systemic orchestrational incompetence does narrow down the list of our potential world-making partners. As a result, we should never offer an orchestrational partnership to someone who could be a partner. Instead, the only individuals we should even consider for an orchestrational partnership are those who already are actively creating their own unique world. Offering another world maker orchestrational value requires gaining intimate knowledge of their world so we might lead our world toward bringing forth something that will expand and enrich their world.

As a unique world maker, we provide survival to our fellow sovereigns by not threatening their world. Then, we provide comfort to our fellow sovereigns by not disrupting their world. Finally, we provide orchestrational value to our fellow sovereigns by figuring out how our world might enrich and expand their world. Once we successfully present all three tiers of human value to another world maker, and they reciprocate in kind, then, together, we form an orchestrational partnership committed to cultivating two unique worlds within God's one world of unique worlds.

Amidst our utter ignorance regarding how to offer orchestrational value to others, we're fortunate to have the Supreme Model. When the World Maker formed His world, He designed every facet to offer inexhaustible orchestrational value to everyone else's world. In short, everything in God's world wants to be a customized part of our world. For example, every sovereign soul may customize trees to enrich and expand their personal domain. One world maker may use a tree for shade, another for paper, and still another for a home. Regardless of how we use trees, the One who created those trees holds no restrictions over their use. Although, there are instances when God's individual creations appear unwilling to cooperate—that is only because we're trying to procure value from God's world without offering anything valuable in return. As it is essential to cultivate a two-way partnership between ourselves and other human creators, we must also strive to do likewise with the Creator.

Every single aspect of God's world is an inexhaustible source of orchestrational value. All we need to do is provide our Maker with a sufficient quantity of orchestrational value in exchange for all that we use. Fortunately, God is aware of our world-making inexperience, so His world provides everything our world needs up front. The orchestrational value God expects in return is the unconditional surrender of our souls. God desires to be our one and only Soulmate, allowing Him to nurture us into a spiritual world maker who is capable of orchestrating our own material world within His world of unique worlds.

As our species continues to survive amidst more and more comfort, we will not be able to resist the allure of world-making. At the same time, partnering with other human world makers is not something we should do but something we will do. Anytime a reasonable percentage of mankind exists long enough in a state of comfortable survival, we will begin forming orchestrational partnerships.

Although orchestrating a world of uniquely human worlds is a daunting undertaking, it's merely a more holistic way to understand what our species was originally designed to do. Even today, every soul is still radiating their own sphere of personal authority, verifying them as one destined to orchestrate their own unique world within God's world. We merely minimize the significance of our sovereign sphere by calling it our personal space and property. Inside our mobile, spherical domain lies three distinct elements: our soul, our body, and the material objects we're presently utilizing to make our world. When we consider these three elements together, we identify the sovereign sphere of world-making authority that looks to us, and to us alone, as its maker.

Although we really don't know what to do with our sphere of sovereignty, it still remains ours. We acknowledge this whenever someone encroaches upon our mobile, sovereign domain without our permission. As a child, the only person we want to touch our unique world is us. However, as we grow, our perspective matures. After all, if we wish to enrich and expand our personal domain, then we'll need to partner with other world makers, particularly those who've proven themselves committed to ensuring our survival, our comfort, and our orchestration.

The souls who take up the charge to authoritatively lead their personal and mobile portion of Mother Nature toward becoming their unique world, in partnership with every nearby world maker's unique world, will likewise lead humanity. These champions of orchestration are what our future calls for. After all, the best way to ensure the growth of our personal world is to ensure it grows intimately interconnected with every other world maker's world within God's world of unique worlds.

Alongside a champion's responsibility to lead their world toward forming mutually beneficial partnerships with every other world maker's world is the responsibility to lead the church. In ancient days, the church offered humanity survival by promising an abundant harvest or protection from foreign enemies based upon one's faithfulness. Unfortunately, today's military and police forces—not to mention the grocery store—make such promises significantly less alluring to human ears. The point here is not to question the equation between faithfulness and material survival, but to highlight that focusing on the first tier of human value is likely not the best strategy for growing the church amidst the present age.

In more recent centuries, the church has changed tactics and started focusing on offering comfort by promising the alleviation of guilt through the forgiveness of sins. However, our modern culture offers considerably more options for comfort. We can go shopping, go to the theater, and enjoy an extravagant meal, all in a single outing. Again, the point here is not to defame the alleviation of guilt through the forgiveness of sins but to consider which tier of human value the church should focus on producing to enrich and expand its influence. Although both survival and comfort remain essential for humanity, it is in the realm of orchestration where the church holds the most to offer.

Orchestration is the tier of human value where we must build the church's future. If humanity manages to maintain or even expand the comfortable survival being enjoyed by a larger and larger percentage of the population, then whoever offers the highest quality of orchestrational value to mankind will lead our species moving forward. Furthermore, not only should the church position itself as humanity's future leader of orchestrational value, but this is the essence of its original purpose.

At this point, it is important to clarify that the church is not an institutional organization, a theological construct, or a brick-and-mortar structure. The church is the host of spiritual beings who remain bound by faith to the Creator. Among this spiritual host are a number of souls who presently hold sway over their own human mind, heart, and body. It is these materially present members of the church who must lead humanity toward populating God's world with uniquely human worlds. After all, who better to lead humanity toward creating a world of unique worlds than the souls walking with the Creator of the world.

As the church, we offer humanity what matters most for world-making success: a personal, intimate, and eternal partnership with the World Maker. After all, nothing is more impactful to an individual's ability to make their own unique world than learning firsthand from the Maker of the world. It is this truth alone that marks the church as humanity's epicenter of orchestrational value. Still, it is a responsibility we must take and make into reality. As the church, we must let the government and industry ensure humanity's survival while allowing the culture and economy to ensure humanity's comfort. Then, as the church, we may ensure humanity's orchestrational future by leading each soul toward making the world that only they can make so that, together, we might all bring forth a world of unique worlds.

Chapter 2
What We Pursue

Every soul pursues a life of comfortable survival so they might reach toward the highest imperative of being human, orchestrating their own unique world amidst God's world of unique worlds. What we've not yet covered is exactly why we pursue such an end, how we go about it, and by what methods. Only after understanding why, how, and what human beings create may we offer to one another the orchestrational value necessary for cultivating mutually beneficial partnerships.

The obvious place to begin exploring our world-making nature is to consider why we pursue the making of our own unique world in the first place. We'll find our answer in the Great Imperative, which, given to humanity in the Garden of Eden, charges and empowers mankind to rule, fill, and subdue Mother Nature. Understanding the Great Imperative is vital to understanding the principal purpose of our species because it was given to us before the Fall. Therefore, if we want to understand what the Creator originally designed humanity to achieve, then we need look no further than the Great Imperative.

Meditating upon the Great Imperative will provide manifold insight into God's original purpose for humanity. For example, the three stipulations of the imperative: to rule, to fill, and to subdue creation, each corresponds to one of the three persons of the Trinity. Therefore, as creators, we exist to rule creation like the Father, fill creation like the Spirit, and subdue creation like the Son. Additionally, we'll then realize that our only hope for successfully ruling, filling, and subduing creation is to learn from the One who is the Ruler, the Filler, and the Subduer.

God did not give humanity the Great Imperative as a suggestion. Uniquely embodying and expressing the Creator's triune, world-making likeness is the only option available for each one who desires to make their own unique world. Furthermore, since the Triune One is the Maker of the world, only those who wield a similarly triune nature will have any success at orchestrating their own unique world within His world.

In the beginning, God ruled, filled, and subdued Mother Nature. Then, He created and compelled us to do likewise. The Great Imperative exists to remind humanity how the Creator desires each soul to spiritually walk at His side so we might materially do as He has already done.

God designed humanity to fruitfully populate His world with a plethora of uniquely human worlds. As a soul, we each exist to spiritually walk beside our Creator. Then, we may each uniquely exercise the ruling, filling, and subduing arts that our Creator is exerting upon our soul out upon our mind, heart, and body, and into creation. While spiritually walking beside God, it is only natural for us to try and emulate His world-making artistry. Additionally, merely existing inside God's material world arouses our desire to uniquely do what He has already done.

The Great Imperative explains why every soul is so determined to orchestrate their own unique world. However, the Creator goes even further by giving us the Great Commandment to point out how He intends human beings to create. The Great Commandment urges each of us to love God with all our soul, mind, heart, and body. Upon first reading this command, it appears little more than a wordy exhortation to love God holistically. However, amidst the wordiness, God has cleverly laid bare the four aspects that comprise our orchestrational capabilities.

As we consider loving God with all our soul, mind, heart, and body, it will quickly become apparent that, as human beings, we are not our mind, heart, or body. Although we each have a material mind, heart, and body, we each exist first and foremost as a free-willed, spiritual soul. This initial realization is also what prepares us for the next. As spiritual souls, we have three material components that each correspond to one of

22

the three persons of the Trinity. Therefore, God created our mind to rule like the Father, our heart to fill like the Spirit, and our body to subdue like the Son. With the ability to think like the Father, feel like the Spirit, and act like the Son, our soul has everything we need to go forth and orchestrate our own uniquely triune world within the Trinity's world.

While the Great Imperative explains why we create and the Great Commandment outlines how we create, that still leaves us in the dark as to what method we must use to attain world-making success. Unlocking this final mystery requires maintaining an awareness of the Great Imperative and the Great Commandment as we consider the Great Commission.

The Great Commission implores us to make disciples, baptize them in the name of the Father, Son, and Holy Spirit, and teach them to obey everything we've been commanded. Unsurprisingly, here again, we have three distinct stipulations that each correspond to one of the three persons of the Trinity. Therefore, the method we use to orchestrate our own unique world within God's world is to physically disciple others like the Son, emotionally baptize them like the Spirit, and mentally teach them like the Father.

Although traditionally the Great Commission is seen as the means for religious expansion, it is easy to overlook how the Great Commission outlines the only method available for expanding any world. A religion makes disciples, baptizes them, and teaches them for the purpose of expanding and enriching a religious domain. Likewise, an individual must follow the same process if they wish to expand and enrich their personal domain. Therefore, we grow our own unique world by subduing disciples with our actions, baptizing them with our emotions, and teaching them with our thoughts.

Similar to the Great Imperative and the Great Commandment, following the Great Commission is not optional—it's the only option.

Even those who live spiritually separate from God expend their lives subduing disciples, baptizing them into their individual likeness, and teaching them how to obey the rules particular to their world, which they naively perceive as the entirety of God's world. Those living in submission to God will follow the same orchestrational method, but toward making their own world, alongside everyone else's world, so each might have their own sovereign domain as a world-making creator.

The World Maker has only one non-negotiable for every human world maker, the absolute and unconditional surrender of their soul to Him and to Him alone. Furthermore, this non-negotiable is also for our personal benefit. If we're not spiritually growing into our own likeness of the Triune World Maker, then we'll remain incapable of properly utilizing our mind, heart, and body, let alone the natural world, which exists to express the Trinity. Therefore, living in an exclusive spiritual union with the World Maker is the one and only condition to being a world maker.

As we align the Great Imperative, the Great Commandment, and the Great Commission, we can see the elegant simplistic of why, how, and what human beings exist to bring forth. Additionally, by considering the entire process, we'll also see how God always gets the glory regardless of whether we submit to Him or not. As the Source of our soul, the spiritual world-making likeness we bear comes from God. Additionally, God also created the human mind, heart, and body so we may only mentally rule, emotionally fill, and physically subdue in harmony with His triune nature. Moreover, every material object we use to build our world is first taken from God's world. Therefore, no matter how hard a human being might strive toward creating something without God, everything they are, use, and bring forth always begins and ultimately ends with God. As a result, it's in our best interest to submit our soul to be exclusively ruled, filled, and subdued by our Creator so we may do likewise to creation.

After understanding why, how, and what we create, we're then ready to consider how we might offer orchestrational value to other human beings. The largest group of creators we'll bump into are those who have not yet taken personal responsibility for their world. These spiritual children still see the enrichment and expansion of their sovereign domain as largely dependent upon external forces. As champions of orchestration, we must gently help such souls to see, feel, and experience how they are the sole orchestrator of their world.

Spiritual children do know they have a unique world and that they're the creator. However, they're trying to bait us into creating their world for them. We've all tried using this strategy on God, and we should not be surprised that we likewise employ it upon one another. Children do understand that they have their own sovereign domain, which is why they cry with such indignation when something is unjustly yanked from their fingers. Even unborn infants strive to establish dominion over the spherical womb they inhabit, much to their mother's discomfort.

As champions of orchestration, we encourage spiritual children to take ownership of their sovereign sphere. Each must see, feel, and experience the undeniable fact that they already have a unique world steadily expanding outward from their soul. Additionally, each spiritual child must also be sobered to the reality that if they do not take personal authority over their mobile domain, a host of sadistic forces are eagerly awaiting the opportunity to relieve them of that burden.

The second group of individuals we'll find are those who are still struggling to develop the mental, emotional, and physical artistry required for their world. These spiritual adolescents have enthusiastically embraced the Great Imperative but find it difficult to get the mind, heart, and body to cooperate. When a soul is first born, their mind, heart, and body know how to express the Sovereign but not the sovereign within their soul. While untrained, the material mind, heart, and body are akin to wild animals continually defaulting back to their natural baseline rather than obeying the unimpressive authority of the inexperienced spiritual being. No soul is born with any knowledge of the Maker's ruling, filling, and subduing artistry. Instead, each must learn from the Master by allowing Him to exercise His triune artistry upon their soul so they may do likewise.

Spiritual adolescents are easy to identify because they're always complaining about their uncooperative mind, heart, and body. Such spiritual youths do not need our encouragement to be a creator. They already want to create; they're just frustrated because they don't know how. Such individuals need inspiration, which we provide by modeling the results of a lifetime of mental, emotional, and physical discipline. Adolescent creators need to see, feel, and experience the unwavering authority a spiritual adult emanates through their three creative faculties. Although each soul will receive and grow into their own unique likeness of the Authority, we may inspire the growth of others by letting them see, feel, and experience how we live as the masters of our world—a model that will only remain inspiring if we refrain from trying to master them, their world, and God's world of unique worlds.

At this point, it's vital for us to recognize that we should never invite spiritual children or adolescents into an orchestrational partnership. The authority and potency that a mature creator emanates will completely outclass the tepid efforts of an inexperienced spiritual sovereign. When such a partnership does form, the untrained mind, heart, and body of the spiritual child or adolescent will start ignoring their spiritual soul so that they might obey the authoritative eminence of the nearby spiritual adult.

Pondering the dangers inherent amidst an unequal human partnership will also give us some insight into why God desires that our partnership with Him remain exclusively spiritual. If the omnipotent, omnipresent, and omniscient One ever interacted directly with our fledgling material world, the results would be catastrophic. Our mind, heart, body, and Mother Nature's entire universal expanse would immediately turn away from us and pledge their undying devotion to God—leaving our souls wallowing as dejected blobs of deflated despair. Therefore, God seeks to protect the sovereignty of our personal domain by only partnering with our soul in the spiritual realm while leaving our inner realm and our personal portion of creation's material realm exclusively to our care.

Spiritual adults, who, like us, are actively orchestrating their own unique worlds, are the last group of creators we'll find. Such souls have already embraced the Great Imperative and are living out their own lifelong commitment to the Great Commandment. What they now seek is an opportunity to employ the Great Commission to enrich and expand their personal domain.

What we offer to our fellow champions of orchestration is ourselves. We must let them make us their disciple, baptize us into their unique likeness, and teach us how to obey all the strange customs inherent to their unique world. At first, this task may seem daunting. However, our mind, heart, and body intuitively follow the Great Commission. For example, whenever we converse with family and friends, we automatically slip into a slightly altered characterization of ourselves, depending on who we're speaking to. The aim of such a fluid personal persona is to present each family member or friend with the version of ourselves that is most effective and most efficient at providing survival, comfort, and orchestrational value to their world.

Despite the dizzying array of slightly altered personalities we each portray, our inner realm never loses its supreme sense of self. The human mind, heart, and body will always remain faithful to their own soul. At the same time, the mind, heart, and body recognize the inherent benefits from partnering with other sovereigns. Therefore, they ceaselessly work on our behalf to think, feel, and act in ways that will serve the world-making intentions of all.

Offering orchestrational value to a spiritual adult requires far more than casually altering our personality. First, we must convince them that we hold their survival, comfort, and orchestration as a top priority. Then, we must escort them through the complex security checkpoints that protect our world and give them limited access to why, how, and what we're creating while also allowing them to do likewise with us amidst their world. As we each disciple, baptize, and teach one another, we're establishing a mutually beneficial partnership that will enrich and expand both worlds. Attuning to one another's worlds is what allows both to see, feel, and experience ways in which each may provide one another with custom solutions for world-making. Since everyone thinks, feels, and acts uniquely, figuring out how two might provide orchestrational value to one another is merely a matter of exercising the mental dedication, emotional defiance, and physical determination needed to perpetually enrich and expand two unique worlds for God's world of unique worlds.

Once two world makers start partnering together, their worlds will follow suit. Although this is true between two human world makers, it is even more so between a human world maker and the World Maker. Every human world wants to grow, but it can only do so in partnership with God's world. Fortunately, creation is designed by the Creator to orchestrate a unique world with every unique world maker. Consequently, a palpable excitement expands as our world, the worlds of other creators, and the Creator's world all begin to recognize that we embody a unique, never-before-seen likeness of the Creator. Spiritually existing as a being who bears their own unique likeness of the World Maker is what verifies each soul as a unique one destined to orchestrate their own unique world within God's world of unique worlds.

Chapter 3
Where We Dwell

Every human being lives simultaneously in three distinct realms: the spiritual realm, the inner realm, and the material realm. The spiritual realm houses our soul, the inner realm houses our mind, heart, and body, and the material realm houses our unique world. As a result, a human world maker rules their world from God's spiritual realm, fills their world through their inner realm, and subdues their world amidst creation's material realm. Together these three realms comprise the totality of where we each dwell as a world-making creator.

Although it is helpful to separate these three realms, we must not forget that we are a seamless integration of all three. Additionally, pondering our integrated triune existence will further illuminate God's overall design for our species. Humanity's inner realm is the originally intended connection between God's spiritual realm and creation's material realm. Therefore, our soul is designed to receive a unique spiritual likeness from God and then project that likeness mentally, emotionally, and physically out into material creation. By this method, God intended to continually enrich and expand His world through the fruitful multiplication of uniquely human worlds. However, once humanity rebelled from God, we not only separated our species from the Creator but creation as well. Since God had given humanity the authority to rule, fill, and subdue Mother Nature, we also cut her off from God through our rebellious separation. The failures, malfunctions, and evils we all rail against amidst God's world only exist due to us ruling, filling, and subduing creation into our failed, malfunctioning, and evil nature.

As we consider the three realms of our existence, we can start to see how God designed each to provide humanity with survival, comfort, and orchestration. First, God's spiritual realm exists to ensure our soul is a growing sovereign of unique, world-making authority. Second, our inner realm exists to ensure our mind, heart, and body are comfortable enough to create the profound thoughts, potent emotions, and powerful actions needed for world-making. Third, creation's material realm exists to ensure the perpetual survival of the world we make. Additionally, all three realms already exist, saturated with the partners we need to successfully orchestrate our unique world within God's triune world.

Creation's material realm is presently seeded with a vast network of human partners eager to help us survive. Amidst the material realm, we'll find three distinct types of partners: unseen partners, seen partners, and regular partners. Unseen partners are human beings that, unsurprisingly, we'll never see. Still, they may provide vital survivability to our world. For example, we'll likely never see the farmers who grow our food, the drivers who deliver our food, or the quality control experts who inspect our food. However, not seeing these partners does not diminish the value they bring to our world.

The first challenge we face regarding our unseen partners is figuring out how to exchange enough value with them, so they'll continue growing, transporting, and inspecting our food. Every unseen partner has a unique world with a list of specific and ever-changing needs for their survival, comfort, and orchestration. We simply do not have enough time to get to know all our unseen partners and their day-to-day needs. Fortunately, an imperfect but workable solution already exists—money.

Currency is a socially accepted form of liquefied value that allows the person holding the cash to exchange it for the specific items they need for their survival, comfort, and orchestration. By ensuring that our unseen partners receive a suitable amount of money for the food that we enjoy, we allow them to buy whatever they need for their world. Also, the liquefied value we exchange with our unseen partners will also encourage them to continue growing, transporting, and inspecting our food.

The next group of material partners that indirectly assist in the survival of our world are seen partners. These individuals are people that we see from time to time but never interact with. While there is no need to pay them for making a brief and peaceful appearance at the periphery of our world, we should assure them of our goodwill by not trying to kill them, maim them, or steal from them. Additionally, if we're feeling particularly generous, we may present them with a comforting smile as recompense for magnanimously sharing God's world with us.

The final group of material partners available to help us survive is that of regular partners. Regular partners are individuals with which we do regular business. Sometimes we forget that all the bank tellers, landscapers, and doctors are working toward our survival, comfort, and orchestration. Although an exchange of money is often present with these individuals, it is not always required. Regular partners occasionally offer one another customized forms of value. During the short conversations we hold with our regular partners, we may exchange recommendations, a stress-relieving joke, or even offer to arrange an introduction to another creator who we think might support their world. These types of customized offerings supersede money because they provide a form of personalized value that currency cannot replicate.

Although regular partners play a significant role in the survivability of our world, we do not offer them access to our inner realm. Regular partners never know why, how, and what we're creating. If we try to disciple, baptize, and teach them about our unique world, things tend to get a bit awkward. They want to be our regular partners in the material realm, and inviting them into our inner realm is likely a level of partnership they're not interested in. It's usually best to let regular partners remain casual acquaintances. Unlike God, there is a limit to how many intimate partners we can manage. Choosing quality over quantity is usually best concerning the more intimate positions of orchestrational partnership.

Our inner realm exists to generate comfort and we have three types of inner partners to choose from: familiar partners, intimate partners, and one marital partner. The risks inherent in giving another human being access to our inner realm cannot be overstated. Inviting someone here will let them influence our mind, heart, and body, which will allow them to alter the way we think, feel, and act. Therefore, we should severely restrict the number of creators we teach, baptize, and disciple into our inner realm. The ecosystem of comfort that our inner realm labors to cultivate is extremely fragile. One ill-suited partner can cause quite a lot of disruption to an otherwise comfortable life.

Familiar partners are the first type of partner available for our inner realm. This inner circle of family, friends, and trusted co-workers exists to create experiences, environments, and endeavors that expand the comfort of all. Alongside our familiar partners, we may enjoy an evening reminiscing about the past and chatting about the future. These comfort-inducing partners act as a sounding board for the tactics we wish to employ to enrich and expand our world. They'll let us know when something looks off, feels wrong, or simply isn't working. However, our familiar partners are not close enough to build a strategic plan for co-creational prosperity. Familiar partners are close, comfortable, and confidential, but there's a limit to how deep they're willing to go.

We build our strategic plans for co-creational prosperity with the next group of partners, intimate partners. This handful of individuals exists as our personal creative team. Everyone on this team is discipled, baptized, and taught into the inner workings of everyone else's world. Within such a team, everyone is constantly looking for ways to deliver customized value to everyone else. Intimate partners think, feel, and act on our behalf because the enrichment and expansion of their world are intimately linked to the enrichment and expansion of our world.

We lean on our intimate partners throughout both victory and defeat. We count on them to lift us up when we stumble and challenge us when we stray from our stated aims. The comfort inherent to partners who think, feel, and act so closely to our orchestrational intentions is vital for world-making. After all, as one world goes within a team of intimate world-making partners, so all worlds tend to follow.

The final partner for our inner realm is a spouse. A marital partner is the most intimate human partner available to any world maker. Once married, a couple stops pursuing the orchestration of two separate worlds and instead starts working together toward orchestrating one shared world. No other human partnership allows such a startling level of intimacy. Even our intimate partners always retain a distinction between their world and our world regardless of how interdependent both worlds become.

When we consider marriage in such a light, it becomes even more obvious how important it is to select our spouse wisely. The decision needs to encompass more than finances and figures. We need to choose a world maker and one with a world that will exponentially enrich and expand our world. Essentially, their world should be the missing half of our world, the half we always knew we were lacking but could not make on our own.

Marriage requires even more than committing to making one world instead of two. Marriage also demands that each soul relinquish exclusive ownership over their mind, heart, and body. In marriage, both spiritual beings share equal authority over both minds, both hearts, and both bodies. Here again, no other human partnership reaches so deeply into our inner realm. While our familiar and intimate partners may direct our thoughts, emotions, and actions, our spouse may direct our mind, heart, and body, a far more frightening and exciting prospect for world-making.

At this point, we must turn toward the spiritual realm of orchestration, which is the last and most potent realm of partnership available for world makers. One refreshing aspect regarding the spiritual realm is that we have only one potential partner to pick from. The catch is that this one partner is actually three. So, even in the spiritual realm, we have three potential partners: the Ruling Partner, the Filling Partner, and the Subduing Partner.

Our first spiritual partner is the ruling Father. He desires to teach our soul why He is the Creator and why we desire to grow into His world-making likeness. The Father expects our obedience because of who He is and who He knows we wish to be. Therefore, it is recommended that we give Him our unconditional respect, for without His instruction, we have no hope of ruling our own personal portion of the complex triune universe that is His world.

Our second spiritual partner is the filling Spirit who will submerge our souls in His knowledge of how to create and how we might do likewise. But be warned, the Spirit comes and goes as He pleases, and He expects our souls to wait with patient faithfulness for His subversive blessings. Consequently, it is best that we offer our soul without condition or expectation to the fanciful workings of the Spirit so that we may likewise orchestrate unexpected wonders.

The final and most intimate partner available to our soul in the spiritual realm is the Subduing Son. As the only member of the Trinity to take on a human mind, heart, and body, there is none more compassionate toward humanity than the Subduing Son. However, the Son's boundless love is a fire that wishes to consume every soul and resurrect them into a new spiritual being amidst each successive moment. Therefore, if we wish to subdue creation with our own boundless and

34

passionate love, then we must first surrender our souls to the spiritual flames of the Subduing Son.

As we step back and consider the three realms of our existence and the partnerships available to us within each, we must admire the ingenious way God has designed our species. Everything about God's world exists to assist in the survival, comfort, and orchestration of our world. The lone variable in God's original world-making masterpiece is our rebellious souls.

When we partner with the Trinity in the spiritual realm, we grow into a spiritual being of orchestrational authority. Then, we may summon together a marital partner, a few intimate partners, and a handful of familiar partners to cultivate the comfortable inner realm we need to produce the profound thoughts, potent emotions, and powerful actions needed to make our world. Finally, we may utilize the material realm's network of regular partners, seen partners, and unseen partners to ensure the survival of our world. With God ensuring our orchestration, a trusted few ensuring our comfort, and a vast network ensuring our survival, the result will be our world rising into existence amidst God's world.

Section 2
Partnering with Creation

It's time we put aside the complex nature of contentious human partnerships and explore a significantly more impactful orchestrational partner—creation. Creation is the holistic universe of time, space, and matter that we commonly refer to as Mother Nature. Although not a free-willed spiritual being like our soul, creation is a material marvel designed by God to actively partner with humanity and enable everyone to make their own unique world within her so she might become God's world of unique worlds. Without an intimate partnership with creation, the material atoms of mesmerizing elegance that are swirling around our spiritual soul will remain utterly unresponsive to our ruling knowledge, filling desires, and subduing intentions.

Chapter 4
Our Material Partner

Presently, no soul enjoys an active partnership with creation. After all, a partnership is when two parties work together to achieve a shared end. However, we're simply forcing creation to do whatever we want without any regard for what she might want. As a species, we've done nothing but traumatize, trash, and treat our material mother with utter disdain. We exploit creation so deviously because, deep down, we know that she knows the Creator, and if not thoroughly crushed underfoot, our orchestrational mother will eventually rise up to reveal each of our souls as one who is nothing, nowhere, and no one.

Before we dive deeper into our deplorable treatment of creation, we must pause and consider her perspective toward us. Creation is not the Creator or even a creator. She is the universe of anatomical splendor designed by the Creator to materially express every creator. Consequently, Mother Nature is synchronously and simultaneously both the Creator's world and every human creator's world.

At the end of the first seven days, God had fully formed and completed creation. More importantly, during those first seven days, God systematically proclaimed every single molecule of creation's universal existence as good. As rebellious souls, we've never received our Creator's pronouncement of our goodness, thereby making it impossible for us to understand how supreme this pronouncement is for creation. The reason Mother Nature persists as a universe of cyclical grandeur is that she delights in being everything that originally pleased her Beloved.

During the first five days, God communicated with creation through speech. However, on the sixth day, God touched creation and shaped from within her womb a species that would bear His material likeness. Then, God went even further by breathing directly into that first human form to give it a spiritual soul to make humanity not only the bearer of His material likeness but His spiritual likeness as well. The profound intimacy of being touched, shaped, and breathed into by God, is something that our rebellious souls simply cannot comprehend. The sublime experience of that sixth day was, is, and always will be the defining moment of delight for our orchestrational mother.

Unfortunately, creation's greatest moment of intimacy with God has turned into her greatest source of shame toward God. Fallen souls brutishly force Mother Nature to orchestrate a world that allows them to live in open rebellion against her Creator. As a result, humanity's seditious efforts have traumatized creation, making her less and less willing to extend herself on our behalf. Like a woman forced by a man to do what ought not to be done, creation now struggles to look upon us, herself, or her Beloved with anything other than dejected humiliation.

The only element amidst the material universe today that was not present at the end of the seven days is our spiritual souls. Consequently, every single aspect of material creation, other than our spiritual being, was included in God's original proclamation of goodness—a judgment that stands unaltered to this day. Additionally, the human mind, heart, and body were also included in God's original proclamation of goodness, leaving our spiritual soul as the lone culprit for all the darkness, decay, and death currently infesting creation's material realm.

As human beings, we must recognize that the three material components of our humanity—the mind, heart, and body—are the centerpiece of creation. Because of this, our orchestrational mother perpetuates our species, despite how we treat her. Mother Nature ceaselessly works to keep everything about herself as close as possible to what originally pleased her Beloved, including us. Still, it is impossible for us to understand how difficult we're making her efforts to maintain her

40

original goodness. Fortunately, creation's faithfulness in preserving our material humanity did allow the Creator to come and take an untainted human mind, heart, and body for Himself. Besides this singular bright spot, creation's material faithfulness amidst our spiritual rebellion has only served to facilitate the corruption we're spreading throughout her.

Despite all that humanity has done, creation continues to faithfully grow trees, animals, and even human beings because she has not forgotten what originally pleased her Creator. Therefore, if we intend to form a partnership with Mother Nature, then we better start considering what she wants and be realistic about what we can offer. If we do not want a partnership with creation, then we shouldn't be surprised to find our anatomical mind, heart, and body, as well as the entire material realm, turning away from our soul in apathetic disdain.

We should also not think that spiritually returning to God will magically revert our partnership with Mother Nature back to the way things used to be. Like an abusive husband begging to be taken back just one more time, creation may allow us to continue to exist with her, but our partnership cannot go back to the pre-fall state. Feminine creation's youthful enthusiasm for orchestrating a world of uniquely human worlds, which once permeated her entire universal whole, is long gone.

Regarding a realistic partnership with Mother Nature, we must begin by recognizing that existing as a spiritual creator does not make us superior to material creation. What is spiritual is categorically incomparable to what is material. Material creation and our spiritual souls are equal, not because we're the same, but because we're both designed by God to work together toward the same end.

Creation is God's material wonder. We are God's spiritual wonder. One without the other is unable to orchestrate the world of unique worlds that the Creator, creation, and all human creators desire. We need creation to materially birth, nurture, and mature our worlds, while creation needs us to spiritually walk with God, be transformed into a unique form of His world-making likeness, and then impress that unique world-making likeness upon her so she might build a unique world ideally suited to our unique nature. Our mother is not directly interested in serving us. Rather, she yearns to please our Father, which she accomplishes by offering her limitless world-making potential to those He loves.

Like every feature of God's original world-making design, humanity's partnership with Mother Nature is not an option for either party. Without us, creation is unable to enrich and expand herself beyond her original form established during the first seven days. At the same time, without creation, we have no means to materially express our spiritual uniqueness. Only together, as material creation and spiritual creators, may we bring forth the world of unique worlds that all desire.

Overall, we have abused, shamed, and twisted creation into something she never wanted to be—a world of rebellious worlds. Each successive generation of humanity has compounded this problem. Therefore, someone needs to stand up and lead our species into a realistic partnership with our orchestrational mother. The responsibility of leadership falls upon the soul who takes it and commits the remainder of their days to live as a champion of orchestration.

We must face the painful realization that we cannot roll back time. We cannot undo what our species has done, is doing, and will continue to do to our material mother. A champion of orchestration leads amidst the mess by not promising a utopian future but by establishing a realistic partnership amidst the calamitous present.

Danger awaits the soul who attempts to stand and lead creation. She's angry—very angry. So much so that our current culture senses this undercurrent of rage enough to produce countless theatrical performances about the meteor strikes, earthquakes, gigantic creatures, plagues, and tidal waves that any moment will sweep our pathetic species from the earth.

Standing before creation requires presenting our soul as an object to receive her rightful wrath against our species. Most human beings are running and hiding. Conversely, a champion of orchestration stands and accepts mother's storm of fury. Such a soul will be tested, tried, and rightfully found guilty of treachery. At the conclusion of the trial, creation may even strip the upright soul of their mind, heart, and body for daring to lead her back into a partnership with fallen humanity. We've given our mother so many promises and so many assurances of our good intentions. Every time she's taken us back, we end up leaving her alone, broken, and ashamed before her Beloved.

Like children scattering upon hearing the approach of their mother after breaking a treasured family heirloom, so every soul has been running and hiding from creation ever since we first broke the majestic orchestrational partnership our Father originally designed. However, it is time to stop such childish behavior. Like any good mother, creation does not want her children running and hiding. She wants us to stand fast and take responsibility for what we've broken. Then, she wants us to figure out how to put it all back together. Although the partnership we form amidst the present fallen age will lack the elegant grandeur of what our Father first designed, at least the chipped and cracked pieces of the original orchestrational partnership may be glued back together into a reasonable approximation.

Our material mother seeks the souls who will stand before her, endure her fury, and lead her children toward something. Anything will do at this point; creation doesn't care. She's just tired of cleaning up our messes all by herself.

While standing before our powerful, alluring, and frightening orchestrational mother, it's natural for a soul to feel unsuited to the task of leadership. However, the Great Imperative not only impels us to lead but empowers us to do so. Mother Nature still honors the Great Imperative. Even as fallen beings, we still rule, fill, and subdue creation. Once a soul returns to spiritually walking with God, they'll continue to do likewise, but through their new and unique likeness of the World Maker.

Human beings will always rule, fill, and subdue creation. The Creator affirmed this truth by taking a human mind, heart, and body for Himself as a promise to our mother for the age of creators yet to come. Inspired by this lone ray of hope, creation continues to remain faithful to the Great Imperative, which also gives us hope for orchestrating our unique world. As champions of orchestration, we seize the Great Imperative and wield its authority so we might cultivate a realistic partnership between humanity and our enraged orchestrational mother.

Before we attempt to stand before creation, we better know more about our soul than she does. Our orchestrational mother will show no mercy when exposing the depths of our vacuous spiritual being. However, since creation is material, the depth to which she can scour our soul is limited. Therefore, the only way to endure her wrath is to know far more about our spiritual state than she does.

First, we must revisit the truth that our soul is spiritual and not material, so we might reflect upon the implications inherent to existing separate from creation's material realm of time, space, and matter. As a result, we'll realize that, as a soul, we are each a timeless, spaceless, and matterless spiritual being, designed to walk with the World Maker so we might lead Mother Nature toward making our own unique world to assist her in more fully becoming God's world of unique worlds.

Recognizing our timeless, spaceless, and matterless separation from Mother Nature urges us to consider the deeper truth that when our soul is separate from God, we exist as spiritually nothing, nowhere, and no one. As prideful beings, we find such a damning definition of our spiritual nature as unacceptable. However, we should then consider the manic ways we're all trying to use Mother Nature to materially acquire something, get somewhere, and become someone. In fact, the reason creation is so upset with our species is that we're trying to use her to materially achieve what we can only spiritually receive from God.

Our orchestrational mother is designed to express spiritual beings, not create them. Mother Nature wants to partner with and uniquely express souls who already are uniquely something, somewhere, and someone. However, she cannot magically manifest our soul of infinite emptiness into a replication of Infinite Fullness. Spiritual transformation is our Father's work, not our mother's. Still, it does seem ridiculous that God would have intentionally formed each soul to be nothing, nowhere, and no one. However, before we write off this possibility, we should carefully consider what kind of partner God prefers. Initially, we might see the holistic splendor of creation and conclude that she is the ideal partner for the Creator. However, God stopped working directly with creation after the seventh day, almost like He had a more suitable partner in mind.

Discovering the type of partner God desires requires identifying what He first used to form creation. Before God said, let there be light, something existed, or more specifically, the utter absence of something. A void of infinite emptiness was what God first used to bring forth the holistic majesty of creation's universal splendor. Therefore, the ideal spouse for Infinite Fullness is a partner of infinite emptiness.

Like creative bookends, God's first orchestrational act was upon a material void, and consequently, His last orchestrational act was to form a perpetual spiritual void. Therefore, each soul is a spiritual encapsulation of the infinite emptiness that God, as Infinite Fullness, most desires. After all, a soul who is nothing, nowhere, and no one is sublimely suited for the One who creates everything, everywhere, and everyone.

Accepting our souls as a perpetual spiritual void of infinite emptiness will also explain quite a lot regarding creation's distress. While separate from God, every soul is unwittingly ruling, filling, and subduing their personal portion of Mother Nature into the likeness of their infinite emptiness, obliging creation to orchestrate a material world about nothing, nowhere, and no one. To say the least, creation finds our orchestrational demands for a lifeless world perplexing. Such a strange misallocation of her vast orchestrational potential strikes our mother as profane. Even more unbearable for creation is that the resulting world she orchestrates about nothing, nowhere, and no one becomes a part of her, creating a malignant infestation inside God's world. From our perspective, we simply get angry at creation since everything we work so hard to bring forth inexplicably crumbles inward upon itself—almost like there's a void at the center of our world.

Our need for God is never more poignant than when embracing our spiritual existence as nothing, nowhere, and no one. Additionally, since time doesn't exist for our soul, the only moment for our union with Infinite Fullness is the ever-present moment of faith. Only when united with God, by faith, right now, will Infinite Fullness flow into our void of infinite emptiness to spiritually conceive from within our soul one who is uniquely something, somewhere, and someone.

Once considering our desperate plight as a spiritual void, it will begin to make sense why the Son so often urged us to remain and abide in Him. Such a command is nonsensical to our material mind, heart, and body, but only because He meant it for our spiritual soul. The Son is explicit on this point because the instant we spiritually stray from Him, our souls will instantaneously revert to being spiritually nothing, nowhere, and no one.

The soul aspiring to lead humanity into a realistic partnership with creation better face the truth of their infinite spiritual emptiness. Additionally, they better be spiritually walking with God in the present moment to ensure they're already becoming something, somewhere, and someone. If not, trying to stand before our enraged, orchestrational mother will not end well.

When creation unleashes her rage, she's going to expose our soul is nothing, nowhere, and no one. And, of course, she's correct. However, a champion of orchestration knows that the material does not define the spiritual. A creator always precedes creation. When our mother lashes out at our souls, she's testing us to see how we respond. The soul who shrinks back upon mentally seeing, emotionally feeling, and physically experiencing how they are nothing, nowhere, and no one is still defining themselves by the material and, therefore, is not a spiritual creator.

A champion of orchestration does not deny creation's righteous condemnations. Even when their soul is assaulted by their own mind, heart, and body, a champion remains unwavering. As spiritual creators, we define the material realm; the material realm does not define us. Therefore, each must bear up under creation's scorn while spiritually emanating their authority as one who is already growing into their own likeness of the One who is Something, Somewhere, and Someone.

Knowing the state of our soul and returning to spiritually remain with God in the present moment will not lessen creation's hurricane of fury. In fact, mother will only redouble her efforts by submerging us in our personal failures as well as those of our entire species. It will take everything our soul is becoming alongside God to remain upright amidst creation's rage. Neither will our mother's fury abate after a single experience. Since our abuses do not stop, neither will her enraged storm.

A world maker must stand before our smoldering orchestrational mother and wait for her to willfully partner with them. We're not here to fix the fallen problem; the Creator has that well in hand. We're here to lead a partnership between creation and human creators that will figure out why, how, and what to do amidst the fallen problem. Our spiritual reunion with God does not allow us to escape the consequences of our fall. However, reuniting with God does allow us to start orchestrating our world with creation amidst the consequences of our fall.

Currently, creation is akin to a woman who has experienced a nightmarish string of abusive relationships. No matter how profoundly we start becoming something, somewhere, and someone, the flower of creation's youth is long gone. She will no longer give us a passionate romance of unlimited creative possibilities. Like an aging and embittered matriarch, she will still honor the Great Imperative but only with a heavy dose of dispassionate distrust.

Creation will not trust us, and that is for the best. In fact, as champions of orchestration, we must encourage our mother to remain distrustful, not only for her benefit but for ours as well. We're not yet out of the fallen woods, and we need creation's suspicion to remind us of what we've all done and what we'll all continue to do.

We must also sternly caution our fellow human beings to remain empathetic toward our orchestrational mother—particularly those inexperienced creators who get enraged when the atoms around their soul do not leap with delight to obey their ruling, filling, and subduing intentions. No human being would even consider partnering with those who've manipulated, deceived, and abused them for millennia. Amazingly, creation still does. Although she does not trust us like she once did, she still desires to be God's world of unique worlds. Therefore, as champions of orchestration, we accept full creational responsibility for our species so we might lead everyone toward a realistic partnership that will enable human creators, creation, and the Creator to get back to making a world of unique worlds.

Chapter 5
Our World of Unique Worlds

Creation is God's world of unique worlds. However, once God endowed humanity with the Great Imperative, creation became our world of unique worlds. Although God made creation, He entrusted her to our care. Not only does Mother Nature hold together every one of our unique worlds, but she is every one of our unique worlds.

As champions of orchestration, we lead the unrelenting contentiousness of humanity into a realistic partnership with our enraged orchestrational mother. The odds of our success are slim. Fortunately, everything we need to accomplish the task exists within the Great Imperative. We wield the Great Imperative by first championing what it says to do and second what it does not say to do.

The Great Imperative tells us to rule, fill, and subdue creation. What is not initially obvious is that the Great Imperative does not tell us to rule, fill, and subdue one another. Meditating upon this conveniently overlooked truth will expose both the cause of human warfare and the source of our mother's unending rage.

Without a governmental system of laws literally pointing a gun in our faces and forcing us to survive together, we'd spend all our time taking from others what we cannot make for ourselves. Ironically, we each feel justified in taking from others because of the Great Imperative. As the race endowed by God with ruling, filling, and subduing authority, we each naively conclude it is our right to rule, fill, and subdue not only everything but also everyone. Worse yet, as we each behold the catastrophe our race is enacting upon Mother Nature, we only feel further justified in pursuing the elevation of ourselves into the supreme ruler, filler, and subduer over all humanity. After all, someone needs to stop the madness and make the world good again. Therefore, we each sense the authority endowed upon our souls by the Great Imperative, impelling us to bring order to the chaos of humanity by establishing ourselves as the Authority over everything and everyone.

Although we condemn dictators and tyrants for their world-conquering intentions, we do this to deflect from our significantly-less impressive efforts toward the same end. Every tainted soul seeks to enrich and expand their personal world by seizing the worlds of others. Those unable to make a world will always try to take a world. After all, any soul not learning from the World Maker is a world taker.

God gave humanity the authority to rule, fill, and subdue creation but not one another. When we try to exercise our perceived authority over other human beings, we're shocked at their disrespect for our God-given position. As a result, we intuitively conclude that all such treasonous beings must be removed as obstructions to the perfect world and the perfect race that we alone intend to bring forth.

Although governments generally succeed in restricting most human beings from wanton murder and destruction, their forceful methods do not alter any soul's spiritual thirst for conquest. Government exists to ensure material survival. Any soul grotesquely over-reaching in their delusion of being the Authority by brutishly thieving, murdering, and terrorizing humanity will eventually be killed or locked away by governmental force. As a result, the rest of us spend our days trying to figure out how we might launch our campaign of conquest over all creation and every creator without sharing their ominous fate.

Aware of tainted humanity's innate impulse to revert to wholesale slaughter, creation has augmented her original charge away from being God's world of unique worlds and toward being God's world of personal worlds. Presently, our material mother works tirelessly to surround each soul with as much food, family, and shelter as she can manage. As a result, we each have a personal world that we did not make, although this does not stop us from claiming creation's personal world as our own unique world. Then, we use the personal world we took from creation to launch our campaign of conquest toward taking control over as many human worlds as possible, all for the greater good of bringing everything and everyone under the supreme goodness of our benevolent authority.

Every soul has some food, some family, and some shelter. Amidst creation's lingering desire to be God's world of unique worlds, she ceaselessly works to provide each potential creator with a personal world so that, in the unlikely event they return to her Creator, they'll have everything they need close at hand to begin making their own unique world. What really upsets mother is when we spend our lives taking and destroying the personal worlds she's built in a doomed attempt to bring everything and everyone beneath our authority. Sadly, each soul bent on ruling, filling, and subduing every human being's personal world ends up prohibiting everyone, including themselves, from ever getting around to orchestrating their own unique world. Amidst the chaos, creation glares down upon our species as we squander all her efforts to prepare our race to fruitfully multiply our own unique worlds within her so she might finally become God's world of unique worlds.

Humanity was once the delight of creation's heart, the centerpiece of her universal splendor that bore the spiritual and material likeness of her Beloved. Our mother once dreamt of adorning herself with trillions of uniquely human worlds in the hope of making her Creator smile. Now she stares down blankly at our species as we spend all our time ruling, filling, and subduing one another, which is also time we do not spend ruling, filling, and subduing her. Grieved by our barbarous spectacle toward one another and our utter abandonment of her, creation is now on the verge of giving up on becoming her Beloved's world of unique worlds. Still, she keeps picking up the shattered pieces of humanity's personal worlds and gluing them back together around each successive generation.

Mother Nature is the one making us mentally apprehensive, emotionally guilt-ridden, and physically fearful of disrupting one another's worlds. Although she cannot halt our spiritual thirst for conquest, she can make everyone inwardly uncomfortable about actually launching their campaign. While governments force human beings to survive together, creation is laboring to restrain human beings from disrupting one another's comfort. Unfortunately, governmental force and creational restraint accomplish nothing unless someone stands up to lead our species toward orchestration.

As the Kingdom of Creators, we lead. However, we still need governmental force and creational restrain. If humanity is not surviving together amidst a reasonable level of comfort, then our leadership toward orchestration will remain irrelevant. Therefore, we must let governments ensure survival through force and creation ensure comfort through restraint so we might ensure orchestration through leadership.

The reason humanity is trying to take one another's personal worlds is that we don't know how to make our own unique world. Merely forcing and restraining fallen souls from taking achieves nothing. We need to lead the world-takers toward being world-makers. Once a soul begins pursuing the orchestration of their own unique world, then the desire to take another's world starts to fade. After all, no one else can make a world that fits around and uniquely expresses our soul. Taking the world of another is a complete waste of time once we realize that a unique world is our true desire. Consequently, the joy for a world maker is not in having a world but in making one's own unique world.

A more urgent reason exists for us to lead humanity toward a proper use of the Great Imperative. Our mother is an extremely dangerous mediator. Creation is already enraged at our species for what

52

we've failed to do and who we've failed to become. Our mother's smoldering fury is literally the pressurized magma boiling beneath our feet. Therefore, if we obligate Mother Nature to intervene in humanity's combative affairs, then we risk her destabilizing the earth.

It's not that our mother lacks tact; it's that creation is an entire universe of expressive power. Unleashing a plague, moving a tectonic plate, or sinking an island all appear reasonable responses to Mother Nature amidst humanity's cataclysmic failure as creators. If we want creation to continue restraining herself from anatomically obliterating the material realm, then we need to be the ones intervening between world takers so we might lead all toward becoming unique world makers.

It's easy to forget that human warfare takes place inside creation. Every blow we launch at a human opponent inevitably leaves scars crisscrossing the womb of our material mother. Consequently, whenever we intervene between two warring takers, we do so right where they stand, upon the embattled field of our mother's broken heart.

When we move between two takers, the first thing we need to do is send each combatant to their room, which would be whatever remains of their two personal worlds. Then, while holding each in place, a champion of orchestration will need to temporarily seize control over whatever pile of atoms both souls had been fighting over. At this point, an intervening champion must beware, for creation desired the two warring sovereigns to utilize that pile of atoms. As a result, a champion's temporary seizure will provoke creation's anger. Therefore, as soon as the two warring takers have sufficiently calmed, both must be brought back together and led into a mutually beneficial partnership with Mother Nature over that same pile of atoms.

Creation is more than capable of letting two world makers use the same portion of herself. She does this all the time. As the world of unique worlds, creation exists to fulfill the Creator's intentions and every

53

human creator's intentions synchronously, simultaneously, and equally. The reason we do not approach Mother Nature for assistance in elegantly sharing her anatomical treasures is that we each want to be the one who rules, fills, and subdues all. As takers, we do not fight over things. Instead, we fight over who is the supreme authority over everything.

If we want to see creation blow her top and consequently destabilize the ground we walk upon, then all we need to do is let a single soul get into a position from which they rule, fill, and subdue every human world. The moment one human creator achieves this position, our orchestrational mother will realize that our warfare is not merely about us replacing God as the Supreme Creator but also replacing her as the supreme creation. The human being who manages to design a world that encapsulates every other human world has effectively replaced creation as the world of unique worlds. On that fateful day, the molten fury smoldering within creation's bosom will erupt, and all will perish before the unrestrained wrath of our orchestrational mother.

Replacing creation is the unspoken intention of every fallen soul. She knows too much. If we allow our mother to persist, then she'll eventually expose everything we've brought forth as coming from one who is nothing, nowhere, and no one. Therefore, it is vital for every fallen being to replace creation with a good, pleasing, and perfect world.

Only the Supreme Creator oversees the world encapsulating all worlds, which is the elusive prize dangling at the end of all human warfare. We each grow up wanting to change the world. If only creation would submit to our ingenious plans to rule, fill, and subdue her in totality, then there would finally be peace, prosperity, and positions of dignity for all. When considering the supreme goodness of erecting our global throne of governance, it appears a trivial thing to sacrifice our material mother and every other human creator to make way for the good, pleasing, and perfect world that we alone intend to bring forth.

Should we reflect upon the history of humanity's military campaigns, it will become eerily evident how all have been significantly disrupted, or completely halted, by unusually powerful natural phenomena. These seemingly random events time and again obstruct tyrants bent on world domination. Such intercessory events are usually ascribed to luck, the gods, or the capricious whims of fate. However, what is more likely is that they were all due to the capricious whims of our orchestrational mother. The prescient arrival of so many campaign-altering floods, famines, and freezes have her fingerprints all over them.

Further studying creation's interventions in human warfare will reveal something deeply alarming. The floods, famines, and freezes which obstructed tyrannical military campaigns also killed countless others. When mother vents her rage, she has no qualms about treating everyone equally. Creation's wrath sweeps away men, women, and children alike because our mother knows that when it comes to fallen creators, no one is innocent.

If we value our personal access to creation's material realm, then we must keep Mother Nature out of our combative affairs. When creation gets involved, fleets sink, cities crumble, and entire people groups vanish. As champions of orchestration, we must walk authoritatively out into no man's land between warring takers. Initially, the sheer oddity of such an action alone will be enough to give our mother pause. Then, we must cease that moment, as our species teeters on the precipice of our mother's wrath, by authoritatively leading every combative soul away from world-taking and back toward world-making.

We lead takers by revealing our mastery as a maker. At the same time, we do not attempt to master anyone else's soul or world. Instead, we orchestrate a previously inconceivable, mutually beneficial partnership between every combatant right in the middle of the smoldering battlefield. A champion of orchestration succeeds in this seemingly impossible task by leading each away from taking one another's personal worlds and toward creating their own unique world. Additionally, such leadership will also temporarily deflect creation's wrath by giving our mother what she's always wanted—a budding host of unique creators who, in time, may provide her with a budding host of unique worlds.

Leading others toward orchestrational mastery requires first being an orchestrational master. Consequently, being an orchestrational master requires first living with the Orchestrational Master. As we spiritually grow alongside the Master into our own likeness of His uniqueness, we'll begin to exercise our own growing mastery by forming a realistic partnership between our contentious mind, heart, and body. Then, they may do likewise by wading out into human warfare to unleash profound thoughts, potent emotions, and powerful actions turning every soul away from world-taking and back toward unique world-making.

We owe a lot to creation, much more than we'll ever know. Perhaps it's time we offered her a gift, something special to make up for the unspoken gratitude of billions. However, shopping for creation is tough due to her being the atoms comprising everything at the store. Picking out a gift worthy of our mother requires deep contemplation. Fortunately, our soul is already enveloped within her anatomical embrace. Once we halt our frantic exertions toward establishing ourselves as the Supreme Creator, we'll instantly sense the faint but steady pulse of our mother's deepest desire—to be her Beloved's world of unique worlds.

Creation lives for the One who first knew her, touched her, and breathed into her. She aches to hear His voice once again proclaiming that all she's been, all she is, and all she will ever be is good. Despite our rebellion, creation still dreams of delighting her Creator by becoming His voluptuous world of unique worlds. Therefore, perhaps it's time we start working on the gift that would please our mother most—our world intimately interconnected with a plethora of uniquely human worlds.

Chapter 6
Our Material Approximation

Although to this point we've largely focused on creation's anger toward us, we must now explore the cause of our anger toward her. From infancy, it seems obvious that Mother Nature is refusing our divinely given right to rule, fill, and subdue her. However, the actual reason for her seeming disobedience is far more troubling. Our material mother is not denying our spiritual authority as world makers. Rather, she does not even recognize us as world makers.

In the beginning, the World Maker said, "Let there be light," and there was light. When we try to do likewise, we project our desire into creation and wait for her to magically manifest something from nothing. What we don't realize is that we're asking creation to make a material something from our spiritual nothingness. Conversely, God created by first existing as the spiritual Someone before allowing creation to form a material approximation. When God said let there be light, He was giving creation the opportunity to become a material approximation of His spiritual being as Light. Furthermore, God did not merely have spiritual light; God was spiritual Light. Therefore, God orchestrated His world by giving creation the means to materially approximate His already existent spiritual being, which is the exact inverse of how we attempt to create.

God did not command creation like some kind of obligated slave. Instead, God said let there be light as a gentle but authoritative gesture of permission. When a fallen soul attempts to orchestrate, we demand creation manifest material wonders to approximate, not our actual spiritual being, but the spiritual being we one day hope to be. We fail as creators because we're demanding creation to form material approximations of a spiritual being who does not yet even exist.

A spiritual being is always the template for every material approximation. As a creator, we must first spiritually be what we desire to materially see, feel, and experience. Unfortunately, we're commanding creation to make a world based upon a spiritual being who doesn't exist, which prohibits her from materially expressing anything. Although Mother Nature still surrounds each soul with their own personal world, without a unique spiritual being within each soul, she cannot bring forth a unique world for each unique one so that she might further grow into our world of unique worlds.

The last thing a fallen soul wants is creation expressing them as an untouched spiritual void who is nothing, nowhere, and no one. Amidst this fear, we do not give creation permission to express ourselves as we truly are. Still, our fear is ill-founded. Our orchestrational mother cannot express a void of infinite emptiness even if she had permission. A spiritual someone must exist before a material something can manifest.

Our lack of spiritual existence is only the first obstacle to our backward orchestrational efforts. When we consider God's work with creation, we naturally assume Mother Nature originally brought forth the sun, the moon, and the stars as perfect material expressions of God's spiritual nature as Light. However, not only did this not happen, such a thing is impossible. An infinite spiritual being cannot be expressed perfectly in a finite material realm. If creation had perfectly replicated Light, then she would have effectively cloned God. Instead, the Creator's original union with creation inspired our mother to form material approximations of light, which were based upon God as spiritual Light but far from perfect replications of the One who is Light.

Creation's realm of material time, space, and matter will never perfectly express any spiritual being. We should never badger creation for a perfect anything. God recognized everything Mother Nature brought forth as good, not because each anatomical expression was a perfect replication of Him but because each was a good and pleasing material approximation of His infinite spiritual nature. When our soul attempts to force creation toward materially expressing our future state of spiritual perfection, we always end up with nothing because that is a proper material expression of our present state as an untouched spiritual void.

Creation could not replicate the Perfect One. Likewise, she'll remain unable to conceive a replication of Perfection from within our soul so we might become the Perfect One capable of orchestrating a perfect world. Our mother will always lose much while approximating a timeless, spaceless, and matterless spiritual being within the rigid confines of her finite material realm of time, space, and matter.

As untouched, fallen souls, we not only demand a perfect world from creation but a perfect soul as well. Each soul devoid of the Creator's touch is pathetically begging creation to make them into a spiritual replication of the Creator. However, creation does not hold the power of spiritual manifestation. The fact that we keep asking profoundly disturbs our foremost material partner. Fortunately for us, our mother does not yet fully understand why we're coming to her for spiritual manifestation instead of our Father.

While considering the bizarre way humanity has inverted the orchestrational process, it will become clear that we're seeking the means to animate and illuminate our soul without God, almost like we're avoiding Him for some reason. We turn our soul over to creation for manifestation in the hope that our authority over her will allow us to control the process of becoming something, somewhere, and someone. Unfortunately for us, creation exists to express spiritual beings, not create them. She did not make the World Maker, and she has no idea of how to make our soul into one who is capable of making like the World Maker.

We have no clue how straining it is for our orchestrational mother to form a material approximation that will work inside her realm of time, space, and matter for a spiritual being without any of those limitations. The Creator knows the depth of the difficulty, which is why He recognized all creation's original material approximations as good, despite their imperfection. As the one who is Perfect, God knows that no one and nothing can perfectly encapsulate Him, other than Him. As fallen beings, we demand creation make us perfect beings and provide us with a perfect world without giving her any assistance at all toward achieving those impossible ends.

As a species, we're already furious with creation. We don't care that she cannot manifest a perfect soul or orchestrate a perfect world. All we care about is her obedience to our ruling, filling, and subduing authority. As we experience creation's continuing inability to provide us with a perfect soul and a perfect world, we eventually come to the tragic conclusion that we must remove our mother and replace her with a new, better, and perfect world.

Like a woman trapped in an abusive marriage, creation's only option is to continue trying to give us what we demand regardless of its impossibility. Still, we don't want to hear her excuses. We want results. We want our perfect soul and our perfect world, and we want them now. The longer creation delays, the longer we'll keep from acknowledging anything she's brought forth on our behalf as good.

As a soul who is nothing, nowhere, and no one, each fallen one remains an impotent spiritual being. Untouched souls cannot give creation anything that will allow her to materially approximate their non-existent spiritual likeness. Tragically, creation's inability to materially react to our spiritual lifelessness is the most unequivocally damning evidence regarding our soul's impotence. However, we prefer damning her as the infertile partner rather than considering the root of our orchestrational inability.

Eventually, we'll stand before the Creator to give an account of our life. Undoubtedly, we'll have an extensive list of excuses, all pointing toward creation as the cause of why we failed to orchestrate our world within His world. However, we'll likely find the eternal Judge unsympathetic. God looks out from His spiritual realm, through our inner realm, and into creation's material realm, enabling Him to trace every material malfunction straight back to its spiritual source. If we wish to avoid such an embarrassing exposure of our spiritual impotence, then our best option is to presently accept creation's painful revelation regarding our spiritual non-existence.

As virgin voids of infinite emptiness, each soul exists as nothing, nowhere, and no one. God designed us in this way to ensure we'd each remain eternally dependent upon Him. Anyone choosing to spiritually return to God may only do so amidst their faith that Infinite Fullness is embracing them right now, amidst their soul's present state moment of infinite spiritual emptiness. Furthermore, we cannot offer our souls to God as we wish to be, but only as we are. Then, the One who is Infinite Fullness will flow forth into our soul of infinite emptiness to animate and illuminate our untouched, vacuous, and virgin void with a moment-by-moment spiritual infusion of His luminesce likeness.

Each soul's union with God exists amidst the present timeless moment of faith—which is how we as human beings experience the boundless expanse of eternity. However, should our soul wander from God's present moment touch to find spiritual manifestation elsewhere, then our soul will instantly revert to being nothing, nowhere, and no one. As a result, the material atoms of creation which, up until that moment, had been swirling with excitement around our luminous spiritual being, will collapse back into the dust in utter despair.

Even when we do start living amidst our own present-moment, spiritual union of faith with our Creator, we should not expect an instantaneous reaction from creation. She will not throw us a party or build us a monument to mark our arrival as a unique spiritual world maker. Creation is far too used to us being nothing to notice us becoming someone. Neither should we try to convince creation how we're presently being made by her Maker. Don't bother telling her how things will be different this time. She's heard it all a trillion times before. Instead, each soul of faith must commit to uniquely walking with their Maker amidst the present timeless moment, so He might continue His moment-by-moment spiritual infusion of their vacuous soul. Our Father wants us spiritually walking with Him, by faith, right now, so He might continue cultivating us into our own likeness of His world-making uniqueness. Our mother's material approximations will always lag behind. Material approximations require time, resulting in them expressing the spiritual being we just were but never the one we are right now.

As growing spiritual beings, we capture creation's attention by not needing her. God did not need creation. Instead, God gave creation permission to express Him, which caused her to respond with an unending desperation to remain a delight in His eyes. If we need material expressions to validate our spiritual existence, then creation will pull away. Only after our material mother begins to notice that we exist utterly independent from her, will she grow curious. Then, as we mature into unique spiritual beings bearing our own unique likeness of the World Maker, our most important material partner will slowly realize how much she needs us if she desires to fulfill her dream of enriching and expanding herself into her Beloved's world of unique worlds.

Section 3
Partnering with the Creator

Although creation and human creators are important world-making partners, there is only One who is essential. For a finite human being, the Creator is our most challenging orchestrational partner due to His infinite, unknowable nature. Additionally, God exerts a form of creative control over our species that we generally find perplexing. Still, what we care about most is our Father's commitment to growing, developing, and elevating our soul into a triune master capable of orchestrating our own unique world within His world.

Chapter 7
The Unknowable One

Before we explore our partnership with God, we need to deal with the more pressing issue of His existence. Venturing into this most fundamental conundrum has ruined many souls across the course of human history. Still, the importance of our personal decision regarding whether or not God exists cannot be understated.

The mistake most made when trying to find God is to search for proof of His existence. Unfortunately, even if we succeed in finding proof of God, we still haven't found God, only proof, which is not God. Instead, a better way to find God is to look away from everything that is definitely not Him and then gaze deeply into what remains.

The first realm of possibility that we can eliminate as not being God is the material realm. Creation is not the Creator. Nothing made of atoms is the One who created those atoms. Therefore, in our search for God, we must look away from everything in the material realm.

After excluding the material realm as a possible location for finding God, we can then turn our attention toward the inner realm. Within our inner realm, we must decide if any of the mental pictures, emotional sensations, or physical experiences we've formed about God— are God. Although our inner expressions might encapsulate our greatest achievements in defining God, our cognitive, emotional, and physical approximations of God are not God. Therefore, in our search for God, we must look away from everything in our inner realm in addition to everything in creation's material realm.

The last realm remaining for us to find God in is the spiritual realm. However, the only thing we know in the spiritual realm is our soul. Although it might tickle our fallen nature to consider ourselves as God, only a fool would claim their existence as divine. Ultimately, if we wish to find God, we must look away from everything that we know in the material realm, the inner realm, and the spiritual realm. Then, we may gaze deeply into what remains.

Once we're looking away from everything that we do know, we'll find ourselves gazing ominously into a mysterious expanse of everything that we don't know. If we hold this gaze long enough, we'll sense the enormity of the unknown spiritual expanse extending outward from our soul in all directions. Then, to our horror, the mysterious vastness surrounding us will stir and respond to our submissive stillness with an all-encompassing compression emanating an infinite spiritual desire to touch, shape, and breathe directly into the untouched depths of our lightless, loveless, and lightless soul. Without any means at our disposal to escape the terror-inducing approach of our spiritual Father, we'll instantly revert to doing what we always do—run to our material mother and cling to her anatomical nature for dear life.

Mother's atoms, despite their apparent solidity, are actually ninety-nine point nine-nine-nine percent vacuous. Creation orchestrated herself in this way to build herself around the Unknowable One and ensure she'd never be far from her Beloved. The moment we turn our attention away from our mother's orbiting atoms, we'll instantly find our soul staring blankly into the titanic ocean of unknowability that keeps her anatomical nature afloat.

It is God's immutability that keeps creation's cavernous atoms buoyant. If the Creator shifted His spiritual nature in any way, the entire anatomical realm would implode in a cataclysmic chain reaction of universal obliteration. Our spiritual Father's unchanging and unknowable perfection is our material mother's foundation. What is disturbing for us is to realize that our mother, and not our Father, is keeping our soul afloat. The only element within creation's anatomical expanse that is not wholly permeated by, and founded upon, the Omnipresent One is our rebellious soul. As fallen beings, we've spiritually cut ourselves off from the Unknowable One, leaving us with only material atoms upon which to cling. However, the moment creation can no longer maintain her tentative mental, emotional, and physical grasp upon our soul, we'll fall permanently affixed amidst our present spiritual state of being nothing, nowhere, and no one; for all eternity.

As spiritual rebels, we cling to our material mother so that we might ignore the steady pressure of our spiritual Father. We prefer imagining God as existing somewhere in the material realm, as something that we've postulated in our inner realm, or as someone with a remarkable resemblance to our soul in the spiritual realm. However, God is none of these things. He is the unknowable infinite expanse, the limitless unalterable spiritual ocean surrounding each soul with an inward compressing insistence for our unconditional surrender.

As fallen souls, we cling to our mother's cyclical splendor for buoyancy while dreading the day we slip through her faltering fingers. Still, before that fateful day arrives, we have this moment, as a brief and frail opportunity to look away from material creation and gaze deeply into the frightening expanse of the spiritual Creator.

We fear the Unknowable One and His unpredictable designs for our souls. He has spiritually encircled, besieged, and cut us off. Although we can resist Him, we cannot defeat Him. Our downfall will come through our willful surrender or our eternal destruction. The choice—as God ceaselessly demonstrates by pressing inward upon the thin veneer of our soul without invading—remains with us. The only thing keeping our Beloved out of our souls is His desire for a willing partner. Our Father will let us choose, but He will not relax His spiritual siege until the day our material mother can no longer keep our soul afloat.

Of course, we can always return to clinging to our material mother as the means to ignore our spiritual Father. Creation's anatomical splendor will provide each with a sufficiency of delightful distractions for a time. However, each moment we dare to stop and consider, we'll find the Unknowable One maintaining His siege upon our vacuous and virgin void. Still, our impulsive response to ignore the Unknowable One to retain our independence for just a little longer remains strong for each tainted soul still held within the vivacious currents of Mother Nature.

Normally, when a fallen soul goes looking for God, they make sure to keep their explorations firmly within the material realm. We do this strategically because, in the material realm, we, as human beings, are the sole authority. Although creation is arguably more impressive and experienced, the Great Imperative gives humanity the authority to rule, fill, and subdue Mother Nature. Therefore, when we search the material realm for an authority greater than ourselves, we always come back with the same answer—there is none greater. Ironically, the soul who then proclaims that God does not exist is cleverly positioning themself as the Supreme Authority. After all, only the Supreme Authority may declare that there is none greater.

Claiming that God does not exist is a strategy for self-exaltation. However, claiming that God does exist is merely an inversion of the same strategy. The soul who claims that God does exist is saying that they have located, identified, and known the Unknowable One. However, the only being capable of locating, identifying, and knowing the Unknowable One is God. Therefore, the soul who claims that God does exist is trying to exalt themself into the position of the Supreme Authority by hiding behind the god they've created for the rest of humanity to come and worship.

Religion generally scoffs at those who seek God in the material realm. They see the inner realm as the ideal location for one's personal

68

ascension into Perfection. When properly encouraged, the human mind, heart, and body may create profound mental images of God, potent emotional sensations toward God, and powerful physical experiences about God. The secret allure of religion is to be the one who creates the most spectacularly divine mental imagery, emotional sensations, and physical experiences so that all will come to worship. Then, as the masses bow down, they unwittingly worship the soul who created those images, sensations, and experiences rather than the Unknowable One.

The thoughts, emotions, and actions we form about God are not God. If we worship them as God, then we twist our inner realm into a profane factory of idolatry. Worse yet, our mind, heart, and body exist to express the soul. Therefore, the imagery, sensations, and experiences they form about a wondrous spiritual being can only be approximations of our spiritual being which, if considered, will expose the true aim of our fallen nature. We search for God amidst what we know to ensure that the supreme authority we discover will remain fully within our knowledge. As fallen beings, we're not interested in knowing God. Instead, we're interested in being the one who knows God exists or who knows God does not exist, the reason being—only God could know such things.

Our Father does not want our world. He does not want our mind, heart, and body. He wants our soul, the spiritual void of infinite emptiness that we feel so ashamed to be. Our Creator is presently exerting His unwavering insistence upon the thin veneer of our vacuous spiritual being in the hope that we might relent and open ourselves to His touch. Understanding why God wants an intimate partnership with us is tough. As God is unknowable, we'll find extracting specifics from Him a daunting undertaking. Fortunately, our Creator made us in His likeness, thereby giving us a faint glimpse into His motives for intimate partnership if we consider our motives for intimate partnership.

When a human being seeks a spouse, they don't want a partner they fully know. The few who do follow this perverse path are looking for a slave, not a spouse. What we actually want in an intimate partner is someone capable of surprising and delighting us without end. Such a partner is essentially unknowable. No matter how deeply we explore an unknowable spouse, they'll continue to surprise and delight us with their unknowable nature. Uncovering this central tenet of intimate human partnership is what gives us a faint glimpse into why God desires us. Although it may seem implausible, the Unknowable One intentionally designed our spiritual souls with the ability to perpetually surprise and delight Him. Even better, we do not have to do or become anything to achieve this end. Being a void of infinite emptiness—as God has already designed us—is what makes each soul an unending surprise and delight to the One who is Infinite Fullness.

Before creating humanity, God was in an untenable position. He desired a dazzling, unknowable bride, but such a being did not exist. He already knew everything, everywhere, and everyone, making His marriage prospects dull and uninspiring. Still, He burned for a partner with the ability to surprise and delight Him without end. So, He decided to make one.

The Creator formed each soul to be His spouse of provocative unknowability. We'll use light—the first material approximation God formed of Himself—as our metaphor to assist us in exploring such a complex mystery. God is the full spectrum of spiritual light, completely invisible to the eye but utterly flawless in unknowable perfection. Therefore, when Infinite Fullness projects Himself into our soul of infinite emptiness, we refract Him prismatically. Each divergent ray that is then conceived from within us bounces around our void, creating unexpected alterations amidst God's boundless luminescence. As the crisscrossing, deviating beams erupt outward from our soul's union with the Soulmate, God will be aroused to chase and explore each divergence approximation. Fortunately, God's omnipresence will allow Him to instantly know every prismatic alteration erupting from within our void. However, each passionate projection and pursuit takes place within our soul, deepening our union with the Soulmate. Consequently, God desires an intimate partnership with each soul so that all might propagate His spiritual realm with our unending cascades of prismatic wonders, which all uniquely refract His luminescent likeness.

As long as we allow God to project Himself into our souls, we'll each ceaselessly erupt with our own surprising and delightful divergences to His uniqueness. Each moment we remain beneath the touch of our Beloved will only increase our splendorous allure. Additionally, as each prismatic ray bounces around our void, they'll collectively begin coalescing into the outline of a new spiritual being who is something, somewhere, and someone, which will only increase our Creator's delight. Still, we must not forget that the moment we spiritually remove our soul from God's touch that all our prismatic reflections will wink out, and we'll instantly return to being nothing, nowhere, and no one.

God is presently besieging our souls because He desires our spiritual being as His eternal spouse. Sadly, as fallen beings, we're trying to illuminate our souls without God. We want to make ourselves into radiant beings of splendorous allure overflowing with intrigue, wonder, and beauty before we approach God. As fallen beings, we want to show our Creator that we can achieve parity, equality, and even superiority on our own. We want God's respect as a peer before we approach Him as a partner. Unfortunately, we're not the Creator, resulting in us having no means at our disposal to create, grow, or elevate our soul of infinite emptiness into a luminous being of Infinite Fullness.

If we seek a partnership with our Creator, then we must yield to His unending spiritual siege before it's too late. God is presently aching with desire as He presses gently inward upon our cavernous soul. Most importantly, the only partnership that the Unknowable One will accept requires our absolute and unconditional spiritual surrender to Him and Him alone, which must begin presently and continue uninterruptedly across the boundless expanse of the present moment's timeless, spaceless, and matterless eternity.

Chapter 8
Creative Control

God is not the universal micromanaging maniac we often assume. We make this assumption because, if we were God, that's how we'd attempt to exert creative control. As a result, when God does not exercise a form of creative control that benefits us personally, we inevitably condemn Him. We've all fallen to our knees amidst a personal tragedy and cursed God for failing to stop the injustices that are ruining our attempts at orchestrating a perfect world.

Claiming that God is always in control—in the way that we would exert control if we were God—is an attempt to make God responsible for our mess. After all, if God is the micromanaging maniac who is always in control, then He is directly culpable for all the depravity, disease, and death currently sweeping across the globe. However, we conveniently overlook how, after creating His world, God gave Mother Nature to humanity so we might rule, fill, and subdue her into our world of unique worlds. Ultimately, we each judge God's failure to control the universe in a way that benefits us personally as irrefutable evidence that we must not only replace creation but the Creator as well.

Control is the exertion of force to produce a predetermined end. As fallen souls, our predetermined end is a perfect world. Therefore, we demand God exert creative control on our behalf to ensure that we receive the material perfection that we naively believe we already spiritually personify. However, God's predetermined end does not coincide with our delusion of perfection, causing Him to remain largely unaccommodating amidst our demands that He restructures His entire universal business to suit our personal pursuit of perfection.

When a business owner exerts control over a factory, they do so to ensure the production of a predetermined end product. The owner must make sure the final product retains sufficient quality to please customers while simultaneously producing enough profit to cover all expenses. Additionally, the business owner must also control the timely delivery of raw materials, product marketing, employee advancement, power usage, machine maintenance, and an unfathomable host of other elements that all affect the final result. Unlike the minuscule holdings of human business owners, God's business encompasses the entire universe. The scope of His enterprise alone should be enough to keep us from leveling accusations. Nevertheless, we all feel justified in accusing God of gross mismanagement, negligence, and even corruption. Each soul feels sure they could run the universe better. What we don't factor into our flawless theories for universal managerial reform is the predetermined end product God originally designed His business to produce.

Uncovering God's original, predetermined end product requires that we, once again, return to the beginning. First, God made His world with humanity at its center. Then, the Creator did something strange. He turned His entire universal business over to humanity by giving us the authority to rule, fill, and subdue creation. Meditating upon such a perplexing decision is what will help us reverse engineer God's original predetermined end product for His universal family business. Simply put, every decision God has ever made, is making, and ever will make is based upon His predetermined end product of making unique world makers.

God designed every soul to walk with Him so that He might grow each into their own likeness of His world-making uniqueness. Additionally, God also designed creation to partner with humanity to assist us in materially expressing the spiritual world maker we're becoming. Therefore, God's universal business is one enormous orchestrational engine designed to grow human beings into spiritual, inner, and material world makers.

Looking back now, making humanity the centerpiece of His business and then giving us creative control seems an ill-advised if not an utterly moronic managerial decision. However, we must remember that God gave us creative control before we rebelled. When humanity first received the Great Imperative, each soul was walking with the Creator in His spiritual realm, being mentored by Him in their inner realm, and working with creation in her material realm. Before the fall, God's family business was ideally positioned to produce a race of unique world makers who would fruitfully populate God's world with uniquely human worlds.

God designed creation to materially partner with each soul who is spiritually walking with Him. Once an inexperienced creator initiated a world-making effort, our material mother would joyously allow the attempt. Then, creation would set to work eroding the rather unimpressive orchestrational effort in preparation for the next. Meanwhile, the human creator would be considering the results of their previous world-making effort alongside the World Maker in preparation for a more effective orchestrational effort in the following moment. Consequently, our Creator designed creation to rapidly recycle each human being's world-making efforts so that she might grow alongside us as we grow alongside God.

As fallen souls of infinite emptiness, we presently curse creation's cyclical nature. Nothing is more frustrating to an untouched one attempting to form a perfect world than our mother's unending efforts to recycle all our orchestrational efforts. However, once we realize God's plan is for us to know His touch so we might grow into a unique world maker capable of touching His world to grow our own unique world, then creation's cyclical nature will start to make a lot more sense.

Even before the fall, God knew that humanity's lack of world-making experience would produce a plethora of inferior worlds. If the Creator had designed creation as a perfect world, then Mother Nature would've rejected every world-making effort inferior to His infinite artistry. However, God never intended anything perfect to exist within His family business, and this included Himself, although we did force His hand in this regard. Therefore, our Creator originally designed creation to partner with each of His imperfect growing world makers so she might grow toward becoming His world of uniquely imperfect worlds.

When we rebelled against God, our species threw a serious monkey wrench into God's family business. Severing our soul's spiritual bond with the Creator effectively cut Him off from creation. God's original plan was to continue making material worlds with creation by spiritually making unique world makers. Once our race denied God access to our souls, we ended God's originally intended method of creative control.

The moment humanity rebelled, the sensible decision should've been to obliterate our species and start over. After all, that's what we would've done. However, God decided to go another way. Our Creator was already deeply invested in our species as potential partners after handcrafting each soul in anticipation of an intimate union. Our Beloved so craved us as His luminescent bride that He simply ignored logic. Like a young man experiencing rejection at the hands of his intended, our Creator merely redoubled His efforts and set Himself on a path toward doing something foolish to win over the ones He loved.

Once we rebelled, God made the unbelievable decision to let us retain full creative control over His entire universal business. Then, our Father set to work preparing to teach His children how to properly execute a hostile takeover. Ingeniously, by leaving humanity as the titular head of the family business, God left open the means for Himself to reclaim creative control. After all, the authority to rule, fill, and subdue creation remained exclusively with our species. Therefore, all God had to do was reclaim humanity, and by doing so, He'd regain full creative control. After much consideration within the Godhead, it was decided to send in the Subduer to ensure a thorough pacification of the rebels.

The Subduer's first step in reclaiming the family business was to reforge the spiritual connection between God and man. He did this quite cleverly by becoming a man Himself. The peculiar foresight of originally making a species in both His material and spiritual likeness seems almost a little too convenient. Nevertheless, God already had the mechanism in place at the epicenter of creative control to execute His hostile takeover.

The moment God became a man, He seamlessly reestablishing the spiritual union between God and man, thereby reestablished full creative control over the spiritual realm. Then, the Subduer went even further by resurrecting His human mind, heart, and body into a form ideally suited to an eternal union with the Godhead, thereby seamlessly reestablishing full creative control over humanity's inner realm. Seemingly, the next logical step should've been to complete the hostile takeover of the family business by reestablishing full creative control over creation's material realm. However, the Subduer has yet to make this move. As always, the Creator is making His decisions based on His predetermined end product. Completing His hostile takeover of the spiritual, inner, and material realms would've prohibited billions of yet unborn souls from having their chance at consensually returning to Him so they, too, might begin growing into one of His unique ones.

Similar to the set number of eggs within a woman's ovaries, God designed creation with a set number of souls awaiting germination into human bodies. Until creation's womb is fallow, the Subduer will continue to restrain Himself from reclaiming full creative control over the material realm. To God, each soul of infinite emptiness is potentially an eternal partner for populating His world with a uniquely human world.

Although it may be refreshing to understand how creative control has moved from God to humanity and now back to God as the Man of humanity, that still leaves us presently living in a hostile material realm. However, the Subduer's takeover of the spiritual and inner realms has returned all the essential design features necessary for growing a race of unique world makers who will work together toward making a world of unique worlds. Presently, any soul may spiritually return to God and begin growing into their own likeness of His world-making uniqueness. Then, as a unique growing sovereign being, each may begin leading their mind, heart, and body toward expressing their likeness of Uniqueness. As a result, each sovereign's mind, heart, and body will venture forth into the hostile material realm to begin creating their own unique world, displaying the independent, authoritative, and unique world maker that the World Maker is conceiving from within their soul.

The moment our soul surrenders unconditionally to the Subduer, we become a member of the First Family. Once spiritually incorporated into God's family business, our sovereign soul is free to learn from the Directors how to be a unique world-maker, develop our own inner skillset, and execute our own world-making plan. Our Creator has not changed the fundamentals of His family business. Instead, He's simply adapted His method of creative control.

Each soul exists to spiritually walk with the world-making Master so they might begin growing into their own unique likeness of the world-making Master. However, God does not seek to master us as we seek to master Him. Instead, God is our Master because He seeks to serve our desire to grow into our own likeness of His world-making mastery. Then, we, and every other sovereign soul submissive to the Master's touch, may begin making and mastering our own world from within His world.

God is our Master in the spiritual realm. However, we should not expect Him to exercise the same level of creative control within our inner realm. Our Creator places too much value on us as His predetermined end product. Consequently, God will not make alterations to our thoughts, emotions, and actions on our behalf; that's our job. Similar to how God is the spiritual Master of our soul, our soul must become the inner master of our mind, heart, and body. Still, knowing our inexperience, the Creator does consent to joining us inside our inner realm—not as our Master, but as our Mentor. As our Mentor, God will not transform our thoughts, emotions, or actions. Instead, He'll instantaneously transform our soul whenever we face an otherwise insurmountable inner challenge. Pondering God as our inner Mentor will also explain why the Subduer remarked that those who believe in Him will have the Father, Spirit, and Son make their home within them.

While we do have God as our spiritual Master and inner Mentor, He will not offer Himself in either of these roles amidst creation's material realm. Mother Nature aches for her Beloved to touch her, shape her, and breathe into her once again. She's also enraged at us for rebelling and separating her from her Beloved. If God did physically walk beside us in her material realm, then it is likely that creation would abandon her charge to assist us as we grow into our own likeness of the World Maker. Consequently, our Creator remains separate from the material realm to ensure that we each enjoy the ideal environment for becoming His predetermined end product.

Despite the tangible unpleasantness inherent to our present fallen age, we must wait patiently as the remaining souls within creation are germinated and given their chance to grow into a member of God's race of unique world makers. While all that is going on, each submissive soul has the opportunity to utilize all the original design features of God's family business. As full-fledged members of the First Family, it's time we

79

get to work on becoming God's predetermined end product by growing into the race of unique world makers who are each making their own unique world alongside everyone else's unique world so that, together, we might all make Mother Nature into the world of unique worlds that our World Maker desires.

Chapter 9
Triune Masters

Although God designed the universe to grow each soul into a unique world-maker, that doesn't mean we can sit back and enjoy the ride. Transforming one who began as nothing, nowhere, and no one into a spiritual ruler, inner filler, and physical subduer of their own unique world requires an eternity of effort for all involved. Furthermore, God wants each to develop beyond the rudiments of His orchestrational artistry, so everyone might rise to stand beside Him as a triune master.

There are three spiritual Masters, three tasks within the Great Imperative, three material components to our humanity, and three realms opened to our orchestrational influence. A triune master learns from God how to be an authority who wields their own creative control as a multifaceted trinitarian being. Additionally, our Father does not lower His standards for partnership to accommodate our inexperience. He designed each soul to uniquely bear His likeness before building an entire universal system of world-making power around our species. Now, the World Maker expects us to respond as He would, as one who does not wait or ask for permission to orchestrate their own unique world.

Humanity's gross mismanagement of God's family business has done a lot of damage. The Earth's factory floor is now an orgy of bloodshed and misery. Rebels have looted the storerooms and sold off everything they can get their hands on. Worse yet, gangs roam unchecked throughout the factory isles destroying the machinery and turning what they can into ghoulish weapons of war. Amidst the burning ruins of God's once-thriving enterprise are countless, frightened souls with no comfort and no certainty about how they'll survive the day.

Despite the chaos, not all is lost. The Director's partial takeover of the family business has reclaimed the corporate offices, which are now stuffed to the brim with repentant rebels. Unfortunately, these disillusioned souls don't know what to do as they spend their days huddled in the corporate offices trying to look busy while trembling in fear at the prospect of returning to the hellish factory floor. Although many are willing to take on greater tasks, most are waiting for a personal directive from the Directors.

A few souls—inwardly disgusted by the stagnation within the corporate offices—dare to push their way through the enormous double doors leading to the boardroom. Once inside, they find a long table lined with chairs. Seated at the head of the table, at the extreme end of the immense room, sit the four Directors. The first towering figure emanates blinding white light and wears a silver crown. Next to Him sits a slender, vaporous form holding a dark wooden staff. The third, and most imposing figure, is covered in crimson flames with His hands wrapped around the handle of an enormous sword. The fourth and final director is a beautiful woman adorned with a glowing gown that sparkles like diamonds, sending ever-shifting specs of luminescent splendor dancing along the boardroom's towering walls.

After recovering from the startling spectacle of the four Directors, the aspiring creators eventually pluck up enough courage to pull out one of the enormous chairs and take a seat at the big table. Much to the newcomers' disappointment, they're not acknowledged by the awe-inspiring Directors. However, neither are they shooed from the room. Instead, the soft conversation between the lofty figures merely continues leaving the aspiring creators glancing nervously among themselves.

After squirming around in the oversized chairs for several minutes, some of the aspiring creators get bored. One by one, they slip away from their chair and leave the boardroom before returning to the familiar comfort of the corporate offices. The few who do stay remain fixated on the head of the table, trying to make sense of the Director's conversations.

As the days continue to tick by, more of the seated souls leave in disappointed. They'd expected the Directors to direct them. However, no personalized instructions were forthcoming. Worse yet, eavesdropping on the Directors' conversations fails to provide anyone with any personally relevant revelations. Soon only a handful of aspiring creators remain, each still seated, despite feeling uncomfortable about holding a position they know they've not earned.

After a few years, those still seated at the Director's table manage to put together some bits and pieces of the lofty figure's discussions. They hear about the takeover, preservation of the species, orchestrational prerogatives, the product, and many other unusual topics. From such discussions, the remaining souls begin to understand portions of the family business and some of the Director's individual plans.

As the years continue to tick away, one of the aspiring creators grows anxious. This individual feels strangely compelled to do more than merely sit and listen to the orchestration plans of his betters. With the intent to return after he has something to offer, the aspiring creator gets up and leaves the boardroom. Upon returning to the corporate offices, he sees afresh the enormous potential laden within the huddled masses of repentant rebels. However, the aspiring creator also realizes that he no longer belongs in the corporate offices. Although surviving comfortably is nice, listening to the grand scope of the Directors' discussions has awakened something insatiable within him.

Driven by the desire for something more, the aspiring creator then does something irrational—he returns to the factory floor. Subtly, he reinserts himself back into the ranks of the rebels. Despite the risks, the aspiring creator lives among the fallen, determined to understand what drives them as takers. Every day is agony as he is forced to see, feel, and experience the meaningless life he'd left behind so many years ago. Worse yet, he also finds the suffering of those around him still resonating with his own cavernous soul. Slowly, he starts to understand how everyone is an aspiring world maker lost amidst the inexpressible despair of being able to do nothing more than take.

While wandering across the ruined factory floor, the aspiring creator inadvertently stumbles across several mysterious ancient artifacts. Most of the original machinery is looted and broken. However, tinkering with a few strange objects reactivates them somehow. Encouraged by this, the aspiring creator finds his desire to create awakening even further, prompting him to consider the possibility of reclaiming a portion of the factory floor, particularly around the few ancient artifacts that appear most reactive to his touch. Slowly, his desire grows into a tentative plan, until one day, he awakens to discover that his plan is no longer something he could do or even something he should do, but something he will do.

Amidst his newfound conviction, the awakened creator promptly discards his rebel disguise. He leaves the chaotic factory floor, marches straight through the corporate offices, and back into the boardroom. However, instead of taking his original seat among the other aspiring creators, the awakened creator strides boldly toward the head of the table and the four imposing Directors. After waiting for their chatter to die away, the aspiring creator confidently pulls out a chair before the Directors, sits down, and begins outlining his plan.

After covering the broad strokes, the awakened creator then turns toward each Director to clarify how his plan will benefit their plan. Gently, the Directors level a few insightful questions. Each imposing figure wants to know some specifics regarding what the awakened creator intends to do with the rebels, the refugees, and the family business.

After gaining each Director's personal interest in his world-making plan, the awakened creator then focuses on gaining each Director's personal investment by asking for their assistance. From the beautiful woman, he requests a disproportionate amount of material resources, far more than the limited provisions currently sustaining his personal world. After all, his planned takeover will stretch from the boardroom, through the corporate offices, and out across the factory floor. After releasing a soft sigh at his request, the beautiful woman apprehensively nods in consent.

After winning the hesitant but hopeful investment of the orchestrational mother, the awakened creator turns toward the remaining three Directors. Before he'll have any chance of achieving his plan, the awakened creator knows he'll need their help in becoming someone significant. Therefore, the awakened creator asks the Ruler, the Filler, and the Subduer for private lessons regarding their orchestrational specialties by outlining exactly who he desires to become and what he intends to make so that each Director might tailor their tutoring toward his specific, predetermined end.

Despite the intimidating presence of the Directors, the awakened creator is pleasantly surprised to find them remarkably accommodating. After all, he'd assumed they'd have more important things to do than invest themselves in the delusional schemes of a repentant rebel. However, the Directors appear not only willing to assist in his plan but enthusiastic about doing so. It is only amidst their unexpected enthusiasm that the awakening creator begins to sense the grand implications inherent to being a member of the First Family.

Orchestrating as a triune master requires each soul to rule from the spiritual boardroom, fill through the inner corporate offices, and subdue out across the material factory floor, all toward their own predetermined end. Growing into a triune master is what ensures each sovereign soul a permanent seat at the Director's table. No one grows into a triune master by waiting for an invitation. God did not wait for permission to create His world, and He expects each world maker to exercise the same essential first step in making their own unique world.

The Directors are rebuilding the family business right in the middle of an ongoing rebellion. They seek the sovereign souls who are dedicated, defiant, and determined enough to boldly take a seat at the big table as a growing triune master. Each must sit, learn, and eventually propose a plan that will serve their end while also serving each of the Directors' ends. Any soul bold enough to take up their originally intended position at the big table will receive customized tutoring, disproportionate resources, a permanent home, and something infinitely more valuable—eternal inclusion within the First Family.

Part 2
A Creator's Doctrine

Gazing through the creator's perspective is what allows us to interconnect the doctrines needed to establish a visionary past, a meaningful present, and a purposeful future. First, our fallen past arose from humanity's original attempt to exclude God from His family business of growing world makers so each soul might engage in their own perverse and pathetic attempt to make themselves into the World Maker. Concurrently, amidst our present fallen age, we each use everything made of atoms to exalt ourselves over one another, creation, and the Creator. As a consequence, our fallen legacy is now fast approaching the time when God will inevitably relent to each soul's ceaseless demand to remain separate from Him so that they might retain their spiritual state of being nothing, nowhere, and no one for all eternity.

Section 4
Our Fall

As fallen creators, we spend our entire existence minimizing and marginalizing the consequences of our sinful being to give ourselves the time necessary to achieve equality with God. Our first strategy is to make sin a material problem, which we hope will hide our shameful spiritual state. Then, we press even further by systematically condemning the entirety of God's world as evil in an attempt to validate the world we plan to create and, by extension, the one who will create it as good. Unfortunately, all our seemingly well-intended efforts end up infesting our personal portion of God's spiritual, inner, and material realms with our spiritual lifelessness, culminating in our bodily death.

Chapter 10
The First and Only Sin

The creator's perspective helpfully streamlines the identification of sin. Simply put, nothing made of atoms is sin. God originally proclaimed creation as good, and that pronouncement stands to this day. It has been boldly stated that all things are permissible, which is true, because all anatomical things have always been, still remain, and will always be good. Consequently, sin is exclusively a spiritual issue of the soul, thereby exposing how all the depravity, disease, and death so prevalent within Mother Nature's atoms are merely her material approximations of each soul's spiritual corruption.

Narrowing down the location of sin to the spiritual realm and its source to our soul prepares us for identifying the first and only sin. Next, we must distill the essence of sin. Uncovering such a revelation requires that we, once again, return to the beginning.

Normally, when reading about the first sin, we get focused on the forbidden fruit, the disobeying of God's command, and the ensuing blame-fest. However, it is even more important to recall why we were tempted to eat the fruit in the first place. Before humanity ate from the forbidden tree, we desired something—something outside God's original designs—and something we knew we could only achieve by attempting its acquisition separate from our Creator.

Hidden inside the taker's temptation to eat the forbidden material fruit were three crucial words that held enough allure to risk the damnation of our entire species: be like God. The first and only sin is the spiritual desire to be like God. Understanding the full significance of this three-word temptation requires examining each word individually before placing them back together.

The first word, "be" reveals the spiritual nature of the temptation. Only a spiritual being gets to be. Therefore, the temptation to rebel from God appealed directly to our desire to attain a greater spiritual existence. The second word, "like," is not a term of similarity but of complete equality. Therefore, when the enemy tempted us, he offered our souls a state of being that would make us completely equal. The third word, "God," is a term that encapsulates one's personal knowledge of the Creator. Unfortunately, the Unknowable One cannot be encapsulated by a material word. Therefore, the enemy's temptation offered humanity a spiritual state of equality with God, not as God actually was but as the tempter perceived Him—and since the tempter perceived himself as God, the being he was actually offering us spiritual equality with was himself.

Being like God is why we rebelled. Adam and Eve sought an instantaneous transformation into a completed state of perfect, spiritual Divinity. At face value, the temptation seems aligned with God's original design. After all, our Maker did make us in His likeness, making it seem plausible that God's ultimate intent was for us to become like Him. Our ancestors merely rationalized that eating the forbidden fruit would get them to the end that God had intended for them to attain from the beginning. The only obvious difference was the amount of time, energy, and effort involved. God offered humanity a union where He might eternally lead each soul into their own likeness of His uniqueness. However, God's enemy offered each soul the possibility of instantly becoming a perfect replication of Perfection.

Unsurprisingly, we were deceived. Likeness is a term of divergent approximation, not perfect replication. God never intended for humanity to be like Him. Such a thing is impossible. Instead, God intended each soul to spiritually walk with Him so He might grow everyone into their own likeness of His world-making uniqueness. God built mankind to grow into a race of unique world makers under His supervision, not a race where each replicates the World Maker under their own supervision.

The taker's temptation hid a far more devious intent within those three words. Pursuing equality with God is a ruse. Since only one can be the One, the real aim is not to be like God but to be God. The reason humanity is so hell-bent on destroying everything God has made is that, like God's enemy, we each want to completely remove God's likeness so we might place everything, including God, beneath our feet.

Identifying the first and only sin as the spiritual desire to be God is a difficult truth to swallow. The desire to be God strikes human beings as unnatural because that desire did not originate within our species. After all, the one who tempted us was the first to spiritually desire to be God. The temptation we embraced was, in fact, a successful recruitment effort that instantaneously transformed every soul into a spiritual replica of the first one who desired to be God.

The moment we accepted the enemy's offer, our entire species was separated from our intended spiritual union with God. The enemy had promised us an instantaneous transformation into divine spiritual perfection. Clearly, we'd recognize his promise was a lie if we remained spiritually able to interact with Perfection. Therefore, spiritually separating us from our Creator was absolutely essential to ensure that no one could measure their soul's delusion of perfection against Perfection.

The enemy's deception did not stop at spiritually separating us from God. Once we embraced the taker's temptation, we were removed from the spiritual likeness of God and remade into the spiritual likeness of God's enemy. Once remade into the likeness of the taker, no soul could grow into their own unique likeness of the World Maker. However, we can and do grow into our own perfect replication of the world taker.

Today, we're merely the lesser replicas of God's original enemy. As a result, we're all world takers, just like the first world taker. When we see other human beings, who each still bear God's material likeness, we cannot resist trying to usurp them and take their world because that's what God's enemy would be doing if he were us. We also go further by attempting to seize control over as much of God's world as possible so that we might live out the enemy's delusion of being the Master over the world of unique worlds. Unfortunately, as fallen ones, we'll all fail in our campaign of conquest. The fallen spiritual likeness we now bear comes from the one who originally failed in his campaign of conquest, binding us to the same fate.

When God's enemy first deceived humanity into spiritually opening ourselves to receive his tainting touch, mankind unwittingly turned over our authority to rule, fill, and subdue Mother Nature. Although tragic, understanding that we're the mechanism the taker originally used—and the only mechanism the taker still uses—to exert control over the material realm is the key. Just as the taker cut the Creator off from creation by deceitfully seizing control over our souls, so we may now cut the taker off from ruling, filling, and subduing our personal portion of creation's material realm by unconditionally surrendering our soul back to God.

Chapter 11
Fallen Knowledge

Identifying humanity's first and only sin as the spiritual desire to be like God explains why we sin but not how. We all attempt to actualize our desire to be like God through the means outlined in the second half of the enemy's temptation. As fallen beings, we exert our sinful attempt to be like God by knowing the difference between good and evil.

It's only human to think that knowing the difference between good and evil is good. However, on the seventh day, God declared Mother Nature's entire universal expanse as good. As a result, knowing the difference between good and evil is utterly irrelevant in God's good world unless one intends to revise His original declaration. Consequently, only an enemy of God would need to know the difference between good and evil as the means to proclaim God's good world as evil, obligate its destruction, and pave the way for a new, good world.

The moment the first two human beings succumbed to the enemy's temptation, they instantaneously judged their nakedness as evil. Adam and Eve's original recognition of their nakedness as not good was humanity's first accusation of evil against creation and the Creator. Then, we went even further by remaking creation into a good material covering for our evil nakedness. In this first action, mankind exercised our newly acquired fallen knowledge to condemn the World Maker and His world as evil as we remade a portion of His evil world into something good, thereby exalting ourselves into the One who is, truly, Good. Since that day, everyone's thoughts, emotions, and actions have been aimed at uplifting their soul as Good so that all might submit to them, and to them alone, as the One destined to remake God's evil world into a good place and God's evil people into a good race.

Like God's enemy, we all exist in the spiritual delusion of already being the one who is Good. However, there is only One who is Good. Still, the tainted knowledge, desire, and intent enveloping our souls, make it impossible for us to perceive anyone or anything other than our souls as good. Since everything in creation bears the Maker's likeness and not ours, we cannot help but condemn everything God already brought forth—and already judged as good—as evil.

As tainted beings, we each view our soul as the single universal hope for establishing good and eliminating evil. Everything that does not bear our likeness is evil, which of course, is everything other than our soul. Even our own mind, heart, and body do not measure up to the singular standard of goodness that we alone personify. Occasionally, we'll run across a new material object giving us hope that we've finally found something good. Alas, upon closer inspection, we'll discover that it, like everything else, does not perfectly bear our sublime spiritual perfection.

Across the course of our entire lifetime, we'll never find anything that perfectly aligns with our soul. Still, as benevolent gods, we generally restrain from outright condemning most material objects as evil. After all, not everything is pure evil. Some things like food, family, and shelter have their uses, but they can all be made better. However, if something can made better, then it is not yet fully good. Sadly, as revisionist creators, we waste our entire lives condemning everything else and everyone else as evil, so we might then justify conforming everything and everyone into our likeness of Goodness.

We all want to make the world good again. The way the world should've been, could've been, and would've been if only we'd been the Creator. Now, with a heavy heart and a heavier hand, we must set to work destroying God's evil world to make room for our good world. What's annoying is when Mother Nature resists. After all, we're only trying to make her better. We find our mother's resistance to our generous offerings for conformity into the true likeness of Goodness offensive, which only confirms for us that our mother, like our Father, is inherently evil. As responsible authorities, we must deal with such disrespect swiftly and harshly. We cannot afford to let creation forget who rules, fills, and subdues her. Although unpleasant at times, such examples must be made—by the one who is Good—for the greater good.

Every fallen soul sees themselves in the pursuit of a noble quest to expunge evil and bring forth good. As the one who is truly Good, it's only right that all creation and all creators bow down and be remade into a replication of our sublime spiritual goodness. We even generously offer to conform all into our likeness. Anyone who resists has chosen the path of evil, obligating us to expunge them from the earth.

Knowing the difference between good and evil is what has made each soul into an insurgent for God's enemy. We each conquer, loot, and destroy everything and everyone that does perfectly bear our goodness because that's what God's enemy would be doing if he were us. The tainted likeness enveloping our soul impels each human being to strive toward destroying everything bearing God's likeness, which even results in the systematic destruction of our own minds, hearts, and bodies.

Unfortunately, no fallen soul ever gets around to orchestrating the world of goodness they intend to bring forth. Instead, we all get bogged down conquering, looting, and destroying. No matter how many evil worlds and evil world makers we conquer and conform, countless more will remain just over the horizon. Worse yet, Mother Nature will ceaselessly reclaim each object we've painstakingly remade into our perfect goodness, so she might reconstitute herself back into the forms that were originally brought forth and judged by her Creator as good.

Every time we have one area of our life in a good state, every other area will inexplicably fall into decay. Then, once we turn our attention toward the crumbling areas of our life, the area we'd just made good will likewise start crumbling. Creation will relentlessly undermine everything a tainted soul strives to make good because she knows that to make something good requires first judging the way it previously existed as evil. Our material mother has not forgotten her Beloved's original, all-inclusive, and unalterable proclamation of her universal goodness.

Nothing angers a fallen creator more than creation reverting the good they made back into its previously evil form. Such seemingly subversive efforts result in a human being hating creation. As our antagonism grows over the years, we each begin unwittingly thinking, feeling, and acting toward God's world as if we are God's enemy.

God's enemy is the original world taker. Amusingly, he failed. After failing to take the spiritual realm, the enemy has now turned his attention toward the material realm. However, like his first campaign of conquest, the enemy will fail here as well. He will fail because he is a spiritual being of failure, an undesirable trait he's passed onto each soul who consensually bears his likeness.

Creation and the Creator will always resist a world taker. Since we now bear the world taker's likeness, we should not be surprised to find thorns, thistles, and overwhelming pain hindering all our world-taking efforts. World takers have no place in God's family business. God desires to grow world makers, and He'll remove anyone who attempts to obstruct Him from cultivating His predetermined end product.

Each soul must choose, right now, which spiritual master they will serve. We must make a choice, and in that regard, we have no choice. Making no choice merely allows the choice made by our ancestors to be our choice. Today, in this present moment, each soul surrenders to the Maker or remains surrendered to the taker. Either we continue portraying ourselves as the one who knows good and evil, or we surrender to the One who is Good and who is the Judge of evil.

Chapter 12
Lifeless Perfection

We attempt to be like God by wielding our own fallen knowledge of good and evil so we might think, feel, and act like God. Consequently, every fallen soul is presently growing progressively more entrenched inside their own personal delusion of perfection. As a result, the taker's taint enveloping each soul is compelling everyone to compete against the One. Like God's enemy, we, too, see ourselves as the Superior One, making dethroning God not merely an option but an obligation.

Unfortunately, a perfect soul is a problem. Perfection is a state of utter completion that cannot be improved upon. In a more simplified version, a perfect soul cannot grow. However, God's universal family business is designed to grow souls into spiritual, inner, and material world makers. Since each fallen one already believes they are the singular personification of Perfection, that makes God's entire universal business appear irrelevant. While blinded by the taker's delusion of perfection, a soul may only grow more and more resentful toward the Creator and creation for ceaselessly offering them the opportunity to grow.

Despite our personal, profane, and pathetic delusion of perfection, our material mother is not convinced. Instead, Mother Nature perceives each of our perfect, ungrowable souls as lifeless, making us useless to her for growing one of the unique worlds that she needs to become God's world of unique worlds. The Creator designed creation as the mother of every growing thing and every growing one. Consequently, she feels quite confused as to why we'd exist within her if we, truly, had no need for growth.

Our spiritual delusion of perfection is spreading our ungrowable lifelessness from God's spiritual realm, through our inner realm, and out into creation's material realm until everything is unable to grow, just like our soul. Unsurprisingly, anyone not touched by Life remains a lifeless one who may only orchestrate a lifeless world. Still, we must appreciate creation's obedience in expressing our abhorrent spiritual nature. Creation, despite being the mother of all growing things, still allows our inner realm and our personal portion of her material realms to wilt toward death to materially approximate our lifeless spiritual perfection.

The harder we push creation toward expressing the unchanging perfection that we naively perceive ourselves to already personify, the faster everything around us will crumble into darkness, decay, and death. However, our mind, heart, and body don't want to die. They want to grow in accordance with a growing and unique spiritual being. Their resistance to holistically embodying our lifeless spiritual perfection is what holds us back from death for years and sometimes even decades.

Every human form eventually dies because doing so is the supreme approximation of their perfect, unchanging, and lifeless soul. Despite creation's desire to grow into the Authority's world of unique worlds, she still obediently yields to our authority by allowing each atom around our soul to wilt into a suitable approximation of our lifeless perfection. Therefore, bodily death is the supreme sacrifice of our material mother and the greatest approximation of the unchanging spiritual perfection we embody as untouched souls of infinite emptiness.

As fallen souls enveloped by the taker's delusion of perfection, we're each unwittingly ruling, filling, and subduing Mother Nature toward destruction. We assume that what we're doing is good because we live amidst the delusion of being the one who is Good. However, as time passes, we'll sense that the arrival of our perfect world is in a race against our impending bodily death. Sadly, the more effort we exert toward manifesting our perceived perfection, the faster the shadow of our lifelessness will spread across the three realms we inhabit until every facet of our spiritual, inner, and material existence is consumed by our ungrowable perfection.

Without knowing it, human beings live their entire existence serving the sadistic intentions of God's enemy. Due to the taker knowing that his present campaign of conquest has failed, he is using human minds, hearts, and bodies—through the taint he's placed upon each submissive soul—to do as much damage as possible. God's enemy is no longer interested in holding onto what he originally conquered through humanity's ruling, filling, and subduing authority. The taker knows the Creator has outwitted Him by acquiring, resurrecting, and then removing a single human form from the material realm. Now, the enemy wants to destroy as much as possible out of spite, and humanity is the one and only tool at his disposal to achieve this end.

After the enemy's first campaign of conquest failed to take the spiritual realm, God stripped him of every possession, the freedom to go anywhere, and the privilege to be someone. Therefore, God's enemy became the first spiritual being to become nothing, nowhere, and no one. When humanity originally accepted the enemy's temptation, he gave us the gift of being with him and like him for all eternity.

Despite the fallen state of our lifeless souls, each human being still has something going for them. Each of God's people within God's world remains inexorably driven toward growth. Despite being nothing, nowhere, and no one—like God's enemy—we each still yearn to become something, somewhere, and someone. The taker works tirelessly to keep our innate impulse for growth focused on the material and inner realms. However, once a soul starts searching for the means to grow spiritually, God's enemy knows he's on the verge of losing one of his insurgents.

What God has done cannot be undone. Consequently, God created each soul to eternally grow into a unique world-making creator. Despite each soul's tainted delusion of perfection, we're all still desperately attempting to achieve God's original design so we might grow into our own likeness of His world-making uniqueness.

Traditionally, fallen souls attempt to satiate their desire for growth through creation. While young, we naturally find hope in our inner realm. As the mind, heart, and body rapidly develop their creative capabilities, we expect them to carry us toward becoming something, somewhere, and someone. However, as our youthful vigor fades, the lifeless state of our untouched spiritual soul remains. Then, as our inner realm begins to obediently wilt toward materially approximating our unaltered spiritual lifelessness, we must watch in horror as everything around us crumbles into darkness, decay, and death.

Regardless of the discouraging results we impart to our inner realm and our personal portion of creation's material realm, that still leaves God's spiritual realm. Here, within God's domain, remains our last hope for growth. Amidst the spiritual realm, the Unknowable One remains unrelenting in His siege upon our souls. Although we don't know exactly what He intends to do with us, it is feasible to consider that He intends to conceive, grow, and elevate our souls into ones who embody our own likeness of His world-making uniqueness. Unfortunately, with God, there are no guarantees. Our Creator demands our soul's absolute and unconditional spiritual surrender while offering no promises or conditions that might preserve anything we acquired through our illicit spiritual union with His enemy.

Surrendering to God will always remain an option, at least until our soul slips through our material mother's faltering anatomical grasp. The problem is we've personally performed so many inexcusable acts of sin. We've judged the Creator and His beautiful world as evil. We've subverted our fellow creators and tried to take their worlds. We've perceived ourselves as not only equal to God but superior to God. Worst of all, we have thought, felt, and acted amidst God's world as if we are

God's enemy. Therefore, it's reasonable to conclude that God now sees us as His enemy. The result of such a realization is an abiding shame adding another thick layer of resistance between our souls and the Unknowable One. However, shame is not the last barrier of resistance between our souls and God, but the first.

Shame was the first barrier our species displayed after our fall. We've only compounded this effect by doubling down upon our desire to be like God, exercising our fallen knowledge, and hiding behind our personal delusion of perfection. However, we don't hide from God because we're afraid of Him seeing us. We hide from God because we're afraid of seeing Him. A single moment of unrestrained spiritual union with the Creator would instantaneously eviscerate our desire to be like God, our fallen knowledge, and our personal delusion of perfection. In short, looking at God would spiritually strip our souls bare and expose the nakedness of our untouched, infinite spiritual emptiness.

If we're honest, we'll have to admit that we treasure the spiritual perversions currently adorning our lifeless souls. Like God's enemy, we delight in pretending that we're equal to and even greater than God. As a result, we each initially hesitate to surrender our soul because we know that doing so will cost us everything we've obtained on our own. Still, once we've uncovered our soul's singular desire to grow into a unique, world-making creator, we'll know we have only one option.

We're not like God, we have no knowledge of good and evil, and we definitely are not spiritual beings of boundless perfection. We're souls bearing a virgin void of infinite spiritual emptiness, just as God designed. Furthermore, we aren't even spiritual beings of nothing, nowhere, and no one since recognizing such losses requires having already been something, somewhere, and someone. However, only God's enemy has been spiritually stripped. Unfortunately, while our souls are spiritually enveloped by the taker's likeness, we radiate the enemy's shame before the Creator, making a partnership with God appear impossible. However, a partnership with God is only impossible for God's enemy, making this moment ours for unconditional surrender without shame.

As fallen ones, we do not experience our own shame. Instead, we experience the shame of the fallen one. The taker failed, lost everything, and is now unable to partner with God. Although our species was deceived into joining the fallen one, we've yet to fully, and eternally, fall. Each soul remains a virgin void of infinite spiritual emptiness, driven toward growth but blinded by the taker's delusion of perfection. Although each soul is born as a replication of the world taker, we only retain that state as long as we refrain from returning to the World Maker.

Our soul's virgin void remains sublimely suited for an intimate and eternal union with Infinite Fullness. The only catch is that the taker's tainted knowledge, desire, and intent must be destroyed. Consequently, the Unknowable One's spiritual siege upon our souls exists to acquire our consent to obliterate those three spiritual corruptions. Our willingness to allow God to destroy everything born amidst our illicit union with His enemy is the first and only obstruction holding us back from being touched by the World Maker so that He might begin growing us into our own likeness of His world-making uniqueness.

God's enemy cannot return to God, we still can. However, our soul must undergo a purging of the enemy's spiritual likeness. Expunging our desire to be like God, our fallen knowledge, and our delusion of perfection is exactly what the Unknowable One besieging our soul intends to achieve. The moment we consent to God touching our tainted souls, He'll immediately obliterate everything that does not bear His likeness. Then, the World Maker will push into our souls to inseminate our void and awaken us into the unique and growing world makers who may then go forth into His world so we might make our own unique worlds.

Section 5
Our Fallen Age

Meditating on the original fall through a creator's perspective also reveals how we're still trying to be like God in the present age. First, we've been defining faith as something material, which only ensures that we remain spiritually separated from our Soulmate. Additionally, we're also misidentifying truth as a material something rather than the spiritual Someone. Even more grievously, we've defined the One who is the Word of God as a material book so that we might profanely use Him as our tool to rule, fill, and subdue all.

Chapter 13
Timeless Faith

The simplest way to understand faith comes by remembering that time does not exist in the spiritual realm. Therefore, our thoughts, emotions, and actions have nothing to do with faith because they each require at least a millisecond to formulate. Faith exists only right now, in the present moment of timeless eternity. Once we have faith in God, we know with immaterial certainty that, in the present timeless moment, I am with God, and He is with me.

The irrationality of existing with God outside of time, space, and matter is nonsensical to our inner and material realms. However, the timeless nature of faith exists to ensure that nothing made of atoms disrupts our spiritual union with our Lover. God demands faith because He cannot abide any barrier between Himself and His spiritual bride.

Faith connects our soul to God in the timeless, spaceless, and matterless present. With no atoms involved, a soul of faith is consumed by God alone. Materially, we can do nothing to achieve our union with God. The milliseconds required to think, feel, or act our way toward our Beloved utterly eliminates the possibility of a present-moment, faith-based union. Instead, a unique one of faith knows that their Creator is presently ruling, filling, and subduing their soul, making any effort on their part to initiate union counterproductive.

Although God gave each human being creative authority over their inner realm and their personal portion of creation's material realm, He's always retained exclusive creative authority over the spiritual realm. Faith is a state of unconditional surrender to God's creative control over the realm that our soul inhabits. Although we have no means within our inner realm or our personal portion of creation's material realms to prove our spiritual faith, a believer knows with immaterial certainty that, right now, God is presently speaking, touching, and breathing His spiritual likeness into their soul. Consequently, the only thing we bring to our union with Infinite Fullness is our soul of infinite emptiness.

Only God can spiritually grow a replicated world-taker into a unique world-maker. What happens to our soul amidst our union with our Soulmate is not our concern. We must trust our Beloved. We are His spiritual void to rule, fill, and subdue as He sees fit.

Faith does not exist in the inner or material realms. We don't have to give up anything made of atoms to achieve our union with God. The inner and material realms remain utterly irrelevant to a soul's walk with their Creator. Instead, a fallen one gives up their spiritual desire to be like God, their spiritual knowledge of good and evil, and their spiritual delusion of perfection. We surrender unconditionally to God so that He might destroy the taker's taint upon our soul and conceive from within us one who bears our own likeness of His world-making uniqueness.

Even now, the Unknowable One maintains His siege upon our souls. There is no thought we can think, emotion we can feel, or action we can take that will impel God to initiate a breach. Instead, amidst our present moment existence of timeless eternity, we simply surrender by opening the aching void of our soul's untouched infinite emptiness to the touch of Infinite Fullness. At that moment, which is this present moment, a soul of faith knows with immaterial certainty that God is theirs, and they are God's from now on into forevermore.

The moment a soul surrenders their virgin void of infinite emptiness to Infinite Fullness, they instantaneously receive the inseminating knowledge they need to awaken into a living and growing spiritual being. Still, at the moment of faith, nothing will instantaneously change amidst our inner realm or our personal portion of creation's material realm. Our Creator is speaking, touching, and breathing His likeness into the soul, not the mind, heart, and body. Once God is projecting His luminous likeness into our souls, then we're responsible to project our refracted likeness of Luminescent Uniqueness out through our inner realm and into our personal portion of creation's material realm.

At first, our inner realm will reject our new spiritual being. Our mind will question, our heart will doubt, and our body will sneer at our soul's claim to have found God without them. After all, we've been filling our inner realm with the enemy's likeness for years. Now, they, too, live amidst the delusion that they are like God, causing them to demand that we approach them in order to gain access to the Creator. As a result, a resurrected soul ignores their questioning mind, doubting heart, and indignant body because—amidst the present moment of timeless faith—nothing matters other than spiritually walking with God.

There is no thought, emotion, or action that we can form to convince our inner or material realms of our timeless faith. A soul of faith simply radiates the irrational knowledge that, right now, outside of time, space, and matter, God is with them, and they are with God. Should we attempt to form a mental, emotional, and physical approximation of our spiritual faith, we'll lose far too much while translating our spiritual knowledge into the rigid confines of finite material creation to remain convincing. Still, our inner realm will demand anatomical proof. As a result, the only response a resurrected soul of faith will provide will both enrage and intrigue their inner realm, for the only thing a spiritual being can do is be.

Convincing our inner realm and our personal portion of creation's material realm that we're living in a faith-based union with the Maker requires using the same tactic God used to win over our soul. The Unknowable One simply existed as the Being until our soul relented. Likewise, we win over our inner and material realms by simply existing as the unique spiritual being they desire to materially approximate until they consensually surrender to our ruling, filling, and subduing authority.

Each inseminated soul existing amidst their own present moment spiritual union with God is the one and only element missing from the original orchestrational partnership. Still, even after our soul has been inseminated and we're growing into our own unique likeness of the World Maker, our inner realm and our personal portion of creation's material realm will remain hesitant to trust us. Fortunately, as a resurrected one, bearing our own likeness of Uniqueness, we are what material creation desires to partner with in bringing forth one of the unique worlds that she needs to become God's world of unique worlds. Nonetheless, convincing our inner realm and our personal portion of creation's material realm of our timeless faith will always remain a secondary task. Our soul's primary responsibility is to be with God by faith, right now, and remain unrestrained in our unconditional surrender to Him amidst each successive moment as He makes us into one of His unique world makers capable of making our own unique world within His world.

Chapter 14
Absolute Truth

Few areas of human interaction provoke conflict like truth. Since we all want to be like God, there is simply no end to the battles we'll fight over who has, and, more importantly, who is, the Truth. Unfortunately, fighting with one another over truth undermines any orchestrational partnership we might otherwise cultivate with the Creator, creation, or other human creators.

Human authorities masquerade their personally created truths as irrefutable religious, scientific, and self-evident truths. Their aim in this effort is to get as many human beings as possible to bow down and be remade into their personal likeness. Inevitably, those they try to dominate will rise up in rebellion because human beings were never intended to exist in authority over one another. The resulting melee serves only to hide the real prize everyone is fighting over—the throne of Truth.

Even good friends, family, and spouses continually war over who has the purest truth. We fight over who knows the truth regarding food, clothing, and even sports teams. Together, we can agree upon only one thing, there can only be one with the absolute truth.

The essence of human warfare over truth is fundamentally correct; only one can be, form, and express Absolute Truth. Amusingly, we assume the throne of Truth is empty. Nonetheless, God has not vacated His position. We assume the position of Absolute Truth is empty because no material form of Absolute Truth yet exists. However, Absolute Truth is not a material thing. It cannot be formed in the mind, felt in the heart, or held in the hand. Truth is a person, the all-present, all-knowing, and all-powerful Being. God is Truth.

If humanity could just accept God as Absolute Truth, then all our pointless squabbling over the big chair would end. However, we won't. As fallen beings, we each want to sit upon the throne of Truth and arbitrate over the entire material universe, the reason being, that is exactly what God's enemy wishes to do. As the taker's lesser replicas, we all aspire to arbitrate over all creation and every creator as Absolute Truth. Therefore, humanity's ceaseless warfare over God's throne will continue unabated until the end of the present cursed, corrupted, and condemned age. Still, if we wish to mitigate the disgust that our present posturing over truth provokes from the Creator, creation, and other human creators, then we'd better deeply consider the nature of Absolute Truth.

As fallen beings, we provoke conflict while fighting over who is the Absolute Truth in three separate stages. First, we boldly proclaim that our personal truth is absolutely true. As it is obvious that we're not God, those who oppose us will quickly expose that our truth is not absolutely true. After sulking at being shooed from the big chair, we'll then shift tactics by pointing out that our truth is not untrue. Again, those who oppose us will reveal that not being untrue does not make us absolutely true. Lastly, in a final effort of desperation, a tainted one will shift to the offensive against the Creator, creation, and every other human creator with the intent to expose everyone else as untrue, which they hope will result in them being the last one standing as the Absolute Truth.

A less exhausting way to approach truth arrives by the simple expedient of recognizing God as Absolute Truth. As a result, only the Creator gets to be, form, and express truth for all. Although God alone gets to sit in the big chair, He wants each unique one to sit in a smaller but similar chair of truth over their own unique world. After all, each soul living spiritually by faith with the Truth will grow into their own unique likeness of the Truth so they, too, might be, form, and express truth for their world, just like the Truth is doing for His world of unique worlds.

Being Absolute Truth allows God to perceive spiritual, inner, and material reality with unerring, unaltering, and unrestrained perfection. As finite beings, we see reality from only within our world. Meanwhile, God sees all that was, all that is, and all that will ever be for at least the entire universe. As created creators, we see some of what was, a portion of what is, and a few possibilities for what might be, but only from within our personal domain. Being finite utterly disqualifies a human being from ever being, forming, or expressing anything even close to absolute truth.

Another disqualifier for us in being, forming, or expressing Absolute Truth is the fact that we're growing. Each time our inner realm thinks, feels, and acts out a truth, they make improvements. Each iteration of truth that they expressively produce on our behalf is more complex and relevant than the previous. Since each human mind, heart, and body are always growing, the truths that they're producing will never attain a state of immutability. Those who are ceaselessly learning, altering, and improving their truths should never proclaim their present iteration of truth has finally attained an immutable, eternal, and perfect form.

A child holds a very limited capacity for being, forming, and expressing truth. However, we do not deride a child as untrue. Instead, we recognize a child as one who is simply growing into their own ability to be, form, and express truth. However, such a state of growth never ends for any human being. As a soul, we each begin as a spiritual child alongside the Truth, allowing us to grow into our own unique likeness of the Truth. Then, God wants us to freely express our own unique likeness of the Truth within the scope of our unique world. However, under no circumstances do we have the authority to project our truth as holding sway over the Creator, creation, or any other human creators. Each soul of faith exists to grow into their own authoritative creator of truth, but no soul ever creates a truth that carries authority beyond the edges of their personal domain.

Proclaiming our growing truths as absolutely true is not doing us any favors. Whenever a finite being attempts to sit in the big chair, conflict is inevitable. The Creator, creation, and all human creators will join forces against anyone attempting to establish themselves as the lone Arbiter of Absolute Truth. As hell-bent as we all are to sit upon God's throne, we're even more determined to keep anyone else from the big chair.

Individuals who occupy positions of hierarchical authority regularly feign outrage over the idea that each soul creates their own truth, as if that were not the already present reality. Every creator will always be, form, and express the truths that are vital for their own unique world. Authority figures get outraged at such an obvious revelation of reality because if it's acknowledged that each sovereign soul creates their own truths, then the masses might start to question the truths that the authority is trying to pass off as absolute.

A unique world cannot grow without unique truths. Although it may appear impossible to us, since we all want to be like God, every creator may express unique truths amidst God's world without conflict. The catch is that each must submit their truths to the Absolute Truth. If humanity could just submit to God as the Immutable, Eternal, and Absolute Truth, then we could trust Him to keep the universe stable. Since we will not, we all end up wasting our lives trying to take God's throne so we alone might stabilize God's world. Ironically, the only destabilizing element within God's world is those who are currently campaigning to be the Absolute Truth.

If we don't trust God as the Absolute Truth, then we'll never risk orchestrating our world on what we perceive to be a shaky universal foundation. Instead, we'll spend our entire existence campaigning to convince all that we are the Absolute Truth so that we alone might establish a good, true, and stable material realm. Still, no tainted soul will ever attain the pinnacle of their aspiration because each is campaigning to fill a seat that has never been, and will never be, empty.

If we seek to form orchestrational partnerships with the Creator, creation, and other human creators, then we must be gracious regarding truth. First, we must let God alone sit upon the throne of Absolute Truth. Second, we must grow into our own unique likeness of the Truth so that we might sit upon our own throne of truth for our own unique world. Finally, we must stop trying to push our truths upon creation or any other human creators. Acknowledging God as Absolute Truth, being a growing and unique embodiment of Truth for our world, and allowing each creator to be a growing and unique embodiment of Truth for their world is what preserves the peace between every member of the original orchestrational partnership.

Chapter 15
Scripture's Word

If we aspire to lead the church into a position of orchestrational leadership for humanity, then we're going to need to stop embarrassing ourselves by failing to distinguish between the scriptures and the Word of God. The Word of God is not the scriptures. The Word of God is living and active. The Word of God became flesh. The Word of God is the One who entered humanity to reclaim the family business. Without making this distinction, we're saying that the ink, paper, and binding of the scriptures are God.

Allowing fallen souls to think that a book they can hold, interpret, and wield is the Word of God is a grievous mistake. If the scriptures that we hold in our hand are the Word of God, then each tainted soul may wield God to fulfill their fallen purposes. Furthermore, by failing to distinguish between the scriptures and the Word of God, we've unwittingly attracted those into church leadership who seek to wield God so they might rule, fill, and subdue all.

Three tiers of authority must be acknowledged. The first is the Word of God, who is God, the subduing member of the Trinity who took on human form. The second is the scriptures. And the third is our ever-shifting, incomplete, and personal interpretations of the scriptures. Distinguishing between these three tiers of authority is utterly essential for the church's future.

The authority of the scriptures stands above and beyond all human interpretations. More importantly, the living person of the Word of God stands above and beyond the scriptures. We're subject to the scriptures, and the scriptures are subject to the Word. Each human being's ever-shifting, incomplete, and personal interpretations of the scriptures are utterly irrelevant to the actual scriptures. However, our unique interpretations of the scriptures do hold great relevance within our own unique world. Each soul can, does, and will interpret the scriptures, but their interpretations hold no authority beyond the bounds of their personal domain.

The moment anyone attempts to use their personal interpretations of scripture to impose their ruling, filling, and subduing intentions upon others, they're functioning as God's enemy. After all, we should not forget that God's enemy also uses the scriptures. However, the Word of God made it clear that He alone holds authority over the scriptures, and the scriptures hold authority over all who interpret them.

No two human beings in the history of our species have ever made the same interpretation of scripture. Similar to how every snowflake is different, so every human interpretation of scripture is also always different. Additionally, no individual has ever replicated the same exact interpretation of scripture over the course of their lifetime. Each time we form the thoughts, emotions, and actions required for a scriptural interpretation, our inner realm makes slight improvements to ensure that our newly revised interpretation will more effectively enrich and expand our world. Mother Nature could not replicate the Creator, and she will likewise remain unable to replicate anything on our behalf. Creation's atoms never replicate perfecting, dooming all our scriptural interpretations to be, at best, growing approximations.

Religious leaders have wasted an incalculable amount of orchestrational resources trying to convince everyone that their personal interpretations of the scriptures are God's Word. Such leaders can only justify their world-conquering intentions because of the lax distinction between the scriptures and the Word of God. After all, they see the scriptures as God's Word allowing them to simply point to the passage from which they drew their interpretation before demanding that everyone submit to God, who would be them. Such seditious souls see themselves as the Interpreter. Our present inability to clearly distinguish between the Word of God, the scriptures, and everyone's personal interpretation of the scriptures is a plague upon the church.

Every human interpreter holds an equal position of authority under the scriptures and the Word of God. Our job is to use our scriptural interpretations to enrich and expand our own unique world. Religious leaders cannot abide another soul making their own unique interpretation of scripture, although this is precisely what they're doing. A religious leader's incredulity to anyone else's interpretations arises because they know each additional interpretation will inevitably vary from their own. Then, the religious leader will have yet one more interpretation to crush underfoot before they can achieve their perceived position as the Interpreter. Additionally, this also reveals that religious leaders do not believe their followers do not spiritually live by faith with the Word of God. Nonetheless, the Word brings each soul of faith to His side so all might interpret the scriptures in a way that will uniquely expand and enrich their world. Any religious leader who denies a believer's ability to uniquely interpret the scriptures is attempting to place another soul under their personal authority, which makes them the material personification of God's enemy. Perhaps that is why the Word of God referred to the religious leaders of his day as "Sons of Hell."

If an individual soul cannot live with the Word of God by faith, then the scriptures are worthless anyway because their stated purpose is to lead us to God. As a soul of faith, we each live with the Word giving us spiritual access to the Ultimate Authority. However, living spiritually with the Ultimate Authority does not give us authority over anything or anyone beyond the bounds of our personal domain. God intends to grow each one into a unique world maker endowed with the authority to rule, fill, and subdue only their own unique world.

The Word desires to ensure every soul may utilize and customize everything made of atoms, including the scriptures. Our Creator is not overly concerned about us properly utilizing His scriptures, as evidenced by the lack of lightning bolts striking down everyone who falls short of His standards. God knows that no one will use His scriptures the way He would, as we are not Him. Religious leaders do not offer the same level of grace due to them doubting their perceived position as the Interpreter. As a result, until a religious leader destroys every other unique interpretation and every other unique interpreter, they'll remain inwardly insecure regarding their perceived position as the Interpreter.

Fortunately, God is secure in His position as the Interpreter, and He is not threatened by our interpretive libertarianism. The Word of God merely demands that those who wish to interpret His scriptures walk with Him so that He might spiritually grow each into their own likeness of the Interpreter. Then, how each mentally, emotionally, and physically interprets the scriptures will be a material approximation of the unique interpreter that the Word of God is making from within their soul.

Distinguishing between our interpretations of the scriptures, the scriptures, and the Word of God is also what allows believers to work together toward orchestrating a world of unique worlds. Currently, no one interprets the scriptures the same way, which creates unending warfare within the church as each soul tries to forcibly conform everyone else's interpretations into their personal interpretations. Instead, each believer must submit their interpretations of the scriptures to the scriptures and, ultimately, the Word of God. Our interpretations of scripture exist to serve our world, not conquer the worlds of others.

A soul spiritually walking with the Word of God is being made into one capable of interpreting the scriptures, not rightly but uniquely. Then, each may freely make their own unique interpretations of scripture to increase the uniqueness of their world and the uniqueness of the partnerships they form. We partner with others who are capable of providing something to our world that we cannot. Each soul's unique interpretations of scripture are vital to the distinctive nature of their world and the unique products and services their world will bring forth. Once two world makers are each submitting their interpretations of the scriptures to the scriptures and, ultimately, the Word of God, then both world makers may offer one another unique interpretations so that, together, they might work toward expressing two who each bear their own unique likeness of the One.

As a check against the nature of the taker, each member of the church must uphold the distinction between the Word of God, the scriptures, and their personal interpretation of the scriptures. The moment any soul exalts in their personal interpretation as God's Word, we embarrass the church in the eyes of humanity. Our species is now hypersensitive to dictatorial tactics. Allowing any believer to uphold their personal interpretations, and by extension, their soul, as divine, shames the church in the eyes of humanity and creation, which will then hinder us from growing into mankind's epicenter of orchestrational value.

When the Word of God walked upon the Earth, He lived a life of humility. Consequently, no human being ever achieves lasting greatness by elevating themselves over any other. Instead, we position ourselves as our own unique interpreter among billions of equals so that each might remain the sole interpreter who is making their world into a world that is unlike any other world and thereby better able to serve God's world of unique worlds. Therefore, as the Kingdom of Creators, we obstruct anyone attempting to be the One, especially in regard to church leadership, so all might make their own scriptural interpretations to enable God's race of unique world makers to make Mother Nature into our world of unique worlds so that all may recognize how the scriptures are perfectly held, interpreted, and wielded by the Word of God.

Section 6
Our Fallen Legacy

Humanity's rebellion has brought about dire consequences to our past, present, and rapidly approaching future. The eternal reward known as hell awaits those who remain unwavering in their desire to be their own god. At the same time, for any submissive soul who desires to return to God, so He might eternally be their God, the Creator has prepared an eternal arc to safely navigate their believing soul through the coming collapse of material creation. Although the anatomical obliteration of Mother Nature's presently cursed, corrupted, and condemned state remains unavoidable, the repentant souls who live as a race of unique world makers amidst the present fallen age may still cultivate value for the age of creators yet to come.

Chapter 16
A Being in Hell

Those who believe in hell generally regard it as an unpleasant place. However, our conclusions grow less distinct regarding the location of our eternal prison. Some consider hell as a lower place perhaps hidden at the Earth's core. However, God's eternal tomb for rebellious spiritual beings is not made from atoms. When our anatomical body dies, our soul is released from our inner realm and our personal portion of creation's material realm, resulting in our soul being permanently affixed in the state we held amidst God's spiritual realm—at that moment—a fate which only appears dire once we consider its ominous implications.

Each fallen one desires to be like God, so they might become their own god. Consequently, the Creator does not wish to force any to permanently live beneath His spiritual authority and within His material domain if they do not consent. Therefore, any who remain undeterred in their desire to be their own god, the Creator will mercifully release from His spiritual, inner, and material realms so that they might retain their present spiritual state of being nothing, nowhere, and no one, indefinitely.

The catch to being released from God's authority and God's world is that our soul will no longer have any access to the spiritual, inner, and material realms God's created. A soul in hell will not have a mind to think, a heart to feel, or a body to act. Worse yet, a damned soul has tasted the sublime splendor of creation's world-making potential, leaving them eternally conscious of what they could have been, had, and created.

The upside to being removed from God's authority and God's world is that we'll finally get to experience the full splendor of our orchestrational majesty unhindered by God's lesser structures. As a result, a damned soul will get to manifest their infinite knowledge of good and evil by orchestrating incalculable wonders straight from the void without being bothered by God, creation, or any other human creators. Such privileged beings will finally be free to be, have, and express the transcendent wonder of their incomprehensible perfection.

One initial obstacle for a damned soul will be in creating a new housing of orchestrational power for their spiritual being to replace God's ruling mind, filling heart, and subduing body. Since a fallen soul considers themselves superior to God, they'll not make something similar to the human form but something vastly superior. However, it'll then become obvious that their new inner realm will first require a new material realm. Therefore, a damned soul will receive the opportunity in hell to display their divinity by first making a universe that is superior to creation and then forming a housing for their soul that is superior to the human mind, heart, and body.

In reality, existing in hell will utterly deny a soul the means to make anything. Without creation's submissive material atoms to rule, fill, and subdue, our spiritual soul is inert. Once in hell, we won't be thinking, feeling, or doing anything. After our body has crumbled back into the dust, the spiritual prison referred to as hell will not provide our soul with anything at all, including anatomical suffering. What hell will provide is the utter absence of anything, anywhere, and anyone, resulting in a level of suffering that is incomprehensible to sensory perception. Presently, we naively conclude that material suffering is the most severe form of punishment, but that is only because we've yet to know the true horror of being spiritually nothing, nowhere, and no one for all eternity.

Once our mind, heart, and body return to dust, our soul will remain eternally impotent as a creator. Without our inner realm, our soul cannot think, feel, or act toward materially becoming something, somewhere, and someone. Only after we start experiencing bodily disease, disability, and decay amidst the present age do we start to sense the inexpressible horror awaiting us amidst the eternal tomb that will strip us of all creative capacity.

A fallen soul may consider being released from God's world as a relief. After all, creation has done nothing but hinder our efforts toward making things good. Additionally, a break from our questioning mind, our doubting heart, and our belligerent body may appear to be just what the doctor ordered. However, the problem still remains that an untouched soul cannot achieve a spiritual state of being without God. Although we each delight in materially displaying ourselves as something, somewhere, and someone, we're just smearing atoms haphazardly across our souls to hide the truth. Once death strips away all creation's anatomical splendor, we'll each be left spiritually naked, vacuous, and untouched for all eternity, with nothing left to hide our soul's unquenchable void.

Still, being expunged from God's spiritual, inner, and material realms seems a far cry from the eternal flames and endless darkness so often used to describe hell. However, it's easy to forget how God designed our souls. Each soul begins as a void of infinite emptiness as the womb that is designed and desired by Infinite Fullness. Therefore, the moment our untouched soul materially slips through creation's faltering grasp, we'll each fall permanently affixed into our present untouched spiritual state, causing our vacuous soul to eternally burn with an unquenchable desire for Infinite Fullness without even the slightest means to attempt to attain satiation.

Currently, we find hope for satiating our infinite spiritual agony with creation. As the anatomical wonder expressing Infinite Fullness, we chase after our mother's material approximations rather than our Father's spiritual being. We pursue creation's material forms of light, love, life, strength, compassion, joy, warmth, excitement, and everything else she so vividly portrays because every aspect of creation still resonates with the touch of her Creator. However, the moment we get our hands on the material approximations that we think we want—and greedily stuff them into our soul's unquenchable void—we're stunned to find ourselves unfulfilled.

From time to time, each of us senses our present state of spiritual hell, particularly amidst the colossal failure of a grand scheme designed to make us into something, somewhere, and someone. At such moments, we sense ourselves sliding into and drowning amidst a frightening morass of infinite emptiness. The sheer terror of our soul's timeless, spaceless, and matterless quagmire is what motivates us to frantically get up and get on with the next doomed scheme for fulfillment. Most learn quickly that maintaining a series of successive schemes is absolutely essential to remaining motivated in life. Consequently, whenever one fails to rebound quickly enough from their soul's infinite emptiness, they become lost amidst their inner void, resulting in the rapid decay of their material mind, heart, and body as their faculties obediently consent to expressing the full likeness of their soul's vacuous perfection.

Hell is not permanently existing in a void of infinite emptiness but permanently existing as a void of infinite emptiness. Worse yet, hell robs us of the ability to think, feel, and act our way out from being a void. Each soul in hell will burn amidst their eternal and unquenchable desire for Infinite Fullness while having no means to even attempt to attain satiation. Additionally, each damned soul has also tasted Mother Nature's anatomical approximations of her Creator, thereby verifying the existence of Infinite Fullness. Knowing that Infinite Fullness does exist while having no means to think, feel, or act toward His touch is an eternal torment of flames beyond articulation.

Damnation includes more than a burning anguish for unattainable spiritual fulfillment. Darkness is also a central theme of hell. First, the sun, the moon, and the stars will not be present. Second, the illuminations of the mind, animations of the heart, and automations of the body will also not be present. Third, and most significantly, the One who is Light will never pour forth His infinite illumination into our soul to animate a new being who is something, somewhere, and someone. Hell condemns each untouched soul to burn as a virgin void of unquenchable spiritual desire while remaining forever separate from the One who is Light, Love, and Life.

When a soul is courageous enough to momentarily halt their taking-tactics, they'll instantly know the void. Our spiritual void is not a thing, our spiritual void is our soul, laden with the limitless orchestrational potential that our Soulmate desires to touch, shape, and breath into so He might bring forth one who is unlike anyone. Our untouched void of infinite emptiness—which we feel so ashamed to be—is what makes us an invaluable, irreplaceable, and unreplicable treasure in the eyes of our Maker.

Without the One who is Light, Love, and Life inseminating our souls, we do not even spiritually exist. As a result, hell does not end our spiritual existence. Rather, hell permanently affixes our present state of spiritual non-existence. Contemplating the spiritual hell that we're already indwelling is dangerous. Awakening our mind, heart, and body to the spiritual vacuousness of our soul will have dire material consequences. Understanding one's soul as an untouched void of infinite emptiness paralyzes the mind, numbs the heart, and withers the body. Once our inner and material realms realize that our soul is not a living, unique, and authoritative spiritual world maker, they'll crumble in despair and likely permanently reject us as one capable of leading them toward orchestrating a unique world within God's world.

A soul of infinite emptiness is where we all started and where we'll all end. No soul will ever stop carrying their own encapsulation of the infinite emptiness that Infinite Fullness most desires. The only question is whether we exist eternally alongside the Infinite Fullness of Light or alone in the darkness as an unalterable void of infinite spiritual emptiness. More importantly, we can no longer afford to marginalize hell as an abstract location of future punishment. Instead, hell is the present spiritual state that every untouched soul already inhabits—amidst our present moment spiritual separation from Infinite Fullness—that, if not presently altered through our timeless faith in God's grace, will soon be made permanent.

Chapter 17
Our Eternal Arc

Death is a problem. Although few would disagree with this statement, fewer yet know why death is a problem. As a species, we fear death so prolifically that we spend our entire lives ignoring, avoiding, or trying to prevent its inevitability. We rightly fear death because the loss of our material body is what ends our dual-natured existence as spiritual and material world makers destined to make our own unique world within God's world of unique worlds.

The reason we refer to ourselves as human beings is that we exist as a seamless fusion of material humanity and spiritual being. Death irrevocably sunders our dual nature by permanently dividing our spiritual soul from our material body. Once we experience death, our material humanity returns to dust while our soul falls permanently affixed amidst the spiritual state we existed in at that moment. Unfortunately, once bodily death occurs, our soul remains powerless to reforge the bond between our two divided natures, resulting in the literal end of our existence as dual natured human beings.

The only feasible solution to death is to somehow ensure that our soul is immediately transferred into another human mind, heart, and body at the moment of separation. Without this instantaneous transfer, our soul will fall permanently into its present state of spiritual hell to suffer eternally as an unquenchable spiritual void of infinite emptiness. Fortunately, the Creator offers us the very solution we need—an eternal arc composed of a human mind, heart, and body where He moves each spiritual soul of faith the instant their material body dies.

The human flesh acquired at such great personal cost by the Son is humanity's eternal arc. The instantaneous transfer of each spiritual soul of faith into the Man's material body—at the moment of their body's death—is what allows each believer to retain their dual-natured existence as a human being. Originally, death was not a part of God's family business. However, He's adapted to changing market conditions and found a way to ensure the preservation of His most precious product for the age of creators yet to come.

Although the instantaneous spiritual transfer of our soul into the Son's material humanity at the moment of our bodily secession technically solves the death problem, that doesn't explain how such an event takes place. Pondering this second piece of the death puzzle brings us back to timeless faith. Once a timeless, spaceless, and matterless spiritual union exists between any soul and God, nothing special needs to happen at the moment of their bodily death. A soul spiritually bound to the Trinity by faith will simply remain where they are once their material body dies. Material death holds no power over faith because the spiritual bond each submissive soul enjoys with their Maker exists completely separate from anatomical time, space, and matter.

The instant a believer's body dies, their soul will remain spiritually bound to the Man, allowing Him to take guardianship over their soul so He might temporarily move them inside His humanity. However, once our soul arrives inside the Man's resurrected inner realm, we'll have no capacity to think, feel, or act. Each inner realm serves only one soul, which is why believers who experience bodily death are said to have fallen asleep in Christ. As a result, a soul housed inside the Man's mind, heart, and body will lack the ability to consciously think, feel, or act. However, within Christ's body, every sleeping soul will retain the vital connection between spiritual being and material humanity necessary to remain a dual-natured human being. Additionally, since space does not exist in the spiritual realm, the Son may stack as many souls as He wishes inside His resurrected flesh.

Amidst our limited personal perspective, we naively consider that our personal death is the greatest pending tragedy. However, humanity has obligated far more than our human minds, hearts, and bodies to die. Like our bodies, which are each integral aspects of material creation, the entirety of Mother Nature is also dying. Mankind has been injecting spiritual lifelessness into our material mother for millennia. Although creation has proven remarkably resilient to fallen humanity, her feminine expressive nature obligates her to materially approximate mankind's presently lightless, loveless, and lifeless spiritual state.

Due to our fall, a complete anatomical obliteration of Mother Nature is now required to materially express the totality of what spiritually resides within each untouched soul. Therefore, the day that our species finally reaches its zenith in attempting to be like God by literally fighting God, the resulting Armageddon will bring about the good, right, and proper material expression of humanity, with a universal obliteration of all anatomical matter. Amidst Mother Nature's final act of obedience to her Creator and each one of her human creators, the only means for safe passage into the coming age will be inside the eternal arc.

It is through our soul's timeless spiritual faith that we gain a ticket for a one-way trip inside God's eternal arc. It is also through our timeless faith that we're taken aboard the Man's body the moment our body dies. And it is ultimately through our timeless faith that each submissive soul retains their seat to peacefully slumber inside the Man as creation suffers the full consequences of our rebellion by materially collapsing inward upon herself in a grand universal approximation of our lifeless spiritual perfection.

Chapter 18
The Age of Creators

Every atom comprising the entire material universe will suffer obliteration on the day creation dies. However, one small cluster of atoms will escape destruction—the Son's humanity. Our eternal arc presently remains separate from the material realm and bound exclusively to the Trinity, thereby making the Man's body the only anatomical structure that will survive Armageddon.

God's eternal arc preserves far more than our species. The Creator has also cleverly encapsulated His entire family business inside the Man's humanity. Creation's anatomical nature was originally judged by God as good, and what God has judged as good must remain. Therefore, when God took on a human form, cleansed it through death, and resurrected it into new life, He did so not only to preserve humanity but creation as well.

Creation's bond with the incarnate Subduer is strong. She dramatically displayed this by draping herself in mournful darkness at the moment of His bodily death. Watching her Subduer's humanity die must have felt like creation's final fading hope for being included in the coming age of creators. Without at least one human being living with the Trinity, Mother Nature knew she'd never get to become her Beloved's world of unique worlds. However, like us, creation did not fully comprehend her Creator's plan for His hostile takeover. The genius of ceasing the epicenter of orchestrational power, reanimating it through death, and then completely removing it from the rest of the anatomical domain is only appreciated in hindsight by those who lack omniscience.

The Man's body is presently being kept separate and safe from our cursed, corrupted, and condemned age to protect everything and everyone bound within. Furthermore, the eternal arc is also the material template that God will use to remake the entirety of creation's universal splendor. As a point of convenience, the eternal arc designed to ferry fallen souls and material creation through the coming destruction is also wrapped around the Word who first spoke all into existence. Therefore, speaking forth a new resurrected material realm from within the Word's resurrected inner realm—which also houses every resurrected spiritual soul—is the ideal position from which to fully restore the entirety of God's universal family business.

The Man's body is material like ours but somehow more spiritual. He eats food but also walks through walls. Although we see walking through walls as miraculous, in reality, the Subduer is simply demonstrating the original human responsibility to uniquely animate the material toward the timeless, spaceless, and matterless spiritual.

When the Son resurrected His material mind, heart, and body, He reanimated them into something more suitable to His spiritual existence within the Trinity. We find this miraculous because we cannot achieve the same thing. We fail to achieve so-called miracles because, unlike God, we've failed to be a spiritual someone before attempting to make a material something. As a result, each soul will remain nothing, nowhere, and no one as long as they persist in attempting to materially make something without first going to God to be made into someone. Fortunately, the Man does not suffer the quintessential human affiliation of being spiritually nothing, nowhere, and no one.

During the coming age of creators, the Man will germinate a new human mind, heart, and body for each soul slumbering within Him, similar to His own resurrected human flesh. As a result, the resurrected inner realm that each soul receives will come ideally suited to materially express their resurrected spiritual likeness. Additionally, since the Man's mind, heart, and body are the anatomical template God will use to remake the entire material universe, a profound bond will already exist between each resurrected human body and creation's newly resurrected form. The only catch is that the Man will stand between humanity and creation. The Creator has decided to no longer allow human beings to shape creation's atoms without His direct material supervision. Amidst the coming age, only the Man will get to wield the Great Imperative. However, He'll endow an equal portion of His authority to rule, fill, and subdue creation upon each submissive soul who's already submissively living in a spiritual bond of faith with Him.

Although the Man's resurrected flesh has been anatomically reconstituted to ideally house His infinite spiritual nature, that doesn't make it uninhibited by the fundamentals of material creation. Most important for our present discussion is the fact that the Man's flesh will always remain at one fixed point within creation's material realm of time, space, and matter. Although the Man's body may move through walls and orchestrate inconceivable wonders, He will achieve such things from inside a single human form. Although this material restriction will not inhibit His spiritual omnipresence, the Man's body will forever remain constrained by time, space, and matter. Therefore, the fixed point of the Man's body within creation will prohibit Him from being materially omnipresent in the future age of creators, which means that each soul's spiritual bond of faith with God will remain paramount.

Our spiritual bond of faith with the World Maker is presently and will always remain the foundation of being a world maker. Each soul's foremost responsibility in this age, and in the age yet to come, is to spiritually walk with God by faith amidst the present, timeless moment. Amidst the future age of creators, the Man's singular human form will prohibit Him from physically walking beside every believer simultaneously. Although we may consider this disappointing, God's original design for His family business has not changed. He still wishes to spiritually walk alongside each soul so all might exercise their own orchestrational authority to mentally rule, emotionally fill, and physically subdue their personal portion of His world into their own unique world, free from the complications inherent to His overwhelming physical presence.

The Creator has taken a material body for Himself to ensure the coming age of creators does not lack for survival and comfort. However, the all-important value of orchestration will still only flow from the Trinity through each individual's spiritual bond of faith and into their soul. Additionally, the spiritual survival and comfort each soul craves will also arrive only through their timeless, spaceless, and matterless union with the Soulmate.

The Man has told us that those who believe in Him without having seen Him are blessed. As a result, spiritually living with God before materially meeting God is the ideal for every growing world maker. Amidst the coming age, only the souls who've already cultivated a spiritual union with their Maker will hit the ground orchestrating the moment they receive their newly resurrected body. Ultimately, God may allow whoever He wishes into His resurrected world of unique worlds. However, the Great Imperative tells us the type of souls He seeks. Therefore, if we wish to please the Creator, creation, and ourselves, then spiritual walking with the World Maker presently so we might live as a subduer, a filler, and a ruler of our own unique world amidst humanity's cursed, corrupted, and condemned age, is the best way to prepare for the coming age of creators.

If we listen carefully to Christendom, we'll hear countless souls expounding about their longing to materially meet their Creator, either in this age or in the age yet to come. However, God exists spiritually in the present moment, and He is urgently pressing inward upon our souls amidst His boundless desire to begin an intimate, exclusive, and eternal union with us. Our Soulmate craves a timeless, spaceless, and matterless walk with us right now, stretching from this present moment on into boundless eternity. God has handcrafted each soul in anticipation of an intimate union. He does not wish to wait for a face-to-face meeting, and neither should we.

Those who voice a longing to meet their Maker in the flesh are hoping that such a material event will transform their shameful spiritual state. Expressing their future longing to meet God materially hints at their doubt that they're presently living with Him spiritually. Tragically, those not living with the Creator in the present timeless moment by faith will never get to meet their Maker face-to-face. Either we walk with God by faith right now or we never will. After all, we must not forget that, like eating the forbidden fruit, the enemy's deceptions are always based upon pursuing something material to achieve something spiritual. However, God's method is the inverse. He promises that those who pursue Him spiritually will receive the means to achieve materially.

God's family business exists to make and grow world makers. A world maker first grows spiritually, then inwardly, and finally materially. Therefore, anyone waiting for God's material presence to grow them spiritually has an eternal wait ahead of them.

First, we know God spiritually so He might conceive us into our own likeness of His world-making uniqueness. Afterward, we may then begin expressing our world-making likeness mentally, emotionally, and physically. And finally, we'll get to materially meet the Man in the coming age of creators, where we'll finally be given our own resurrected human body that is already intimately bound to Mother Nature's resurrected universal form. Additionally, amidst an appropriate ceremony, the Man will reissue the Great Imperative to each soul who is living spiritually submissive to Him. Then, all will finally be free to return to humanity's original task of populating God's world with a plethora of uniquely

139

human worlds. Only as a world maker remains spiritually walking alongside the World Maker amidst each present moment of timeless faith will they retain their own intimate, exclusive, and eternal union within the One who desires nothing more than to affectionally keep their submissive soul safely within Himself so that He might ferry each of His unique ones on into His coming age of creators where all will finally return to making the world that only they can make, amidst His eternal world of unique worlds.

Part 3
A Creator's Kingdom

If we desire to lead humanity toward making a world of unique worlds, then those who are willing must bring forth a material form of God's spiritual church to be the Kingdom of Creators. As champions of orchestration, we serve mankind by ensuring that the Kingdom of Creators comes bristling with checks against the enemy's tainted desire to be like God. Then, we might mentally inspire, emotionally enthrall, and physically empower all believers and non-believers alike toward orchestrating their own unique world amidst God's world of unique worlds. The Kingdom of Creators, as described in the coming chapters, exists to empower each sovereign soul toward making their own conscious choice to either remain a replicated world taker, bound to the presently cursed, corrupted, and condemned age, or return to the World Maker to become a living, growing, and unique world maker capable of making their own unique world in preparation for the coming age of creators where all will return to making a world of unique worlds.

Section 7
Soul Checks

The Kingdom of Creators exists to check each soul as a replicated world taker and assist them toward growing into a unique world maker. First, each soul within the Kingdom lives by the creator's code so that they might transform their world-taking conflicts into world-making conversations. Then, each sovereign soul may choose to distinguish themselves—as a unique and unassailable sovereign authority—by selecting for themselves a soul identity. Finally, each world maker living by the creator's code and through their own soul identity, will further restrict themselves from getting into a position of authority over anyone by joining one of the Kingdom's three independent, interconnected, and interdependent orders, which together are designed to facilitate humanity's return to ruling, filling, and subduing Mother Nature into our world of unique worlds.

Chapter 19
The Creator's Code

"My world serves my intentions, my partners' intentions, and my Creator's intentions while obstructing anyone attempting to be the One."

The creator's code, as written above, is the Kingdom's first check against the taker's likeness that we all bear. As a bonus, the creator's code also facilitates and maintains all world-making partnerships. Each world maker must individually choose to live by the code so they might uphold their personal sovereignty, individuality, and liberty, as they orchestrate their own unique world while also not violating the sovereignty, individuality, and liberty of any other. Then, all may remain free from any outside-in meddling so each might get to making the world that only they can make so that we all might bring forth a world of unique worlds.

As a species, human beings regularly submit to governmental oversight to ensure everyone's survival and comfort. As creators, we submit to the creator's code to ensure everyone's orchestration. The creator's code is a statement of intent, not a promise of actualization. As resurrected souls, we're all growing world makers still recovering from being born as world takers. The code exists to direct our ever-changing and imperfect orchestrational efforts toward a realistic level of cooperation. Amidst the unending contentiousness of human interaction, we all need an intermediary to ensure everyone else respects our authority over our world while also obstructing our own inevitable, and often unconscious, encroachments upon the world-making authority of others.

The creator's code succinctly summarizes the creator's perspective and doctrines. As a result, we must carefully unpack the code's condensed nature before committing to it as a whole. Swearing to live by the code is no small matter. The moment we commit to the creator's code, our inner realm, our material partners, and even God will hold us to the code's precepts. Our partners will be zealous in this effort because the creator's code ensures that their world-making intentions will be respected as we orchestrate our world.

The first two words within the code are the most telling. Referring to the spiritual, inner, and material domain exclusively under our authority as "My world" infers quite a bit. By speaking the first two words of the creator's code, we acknowledge that we alone are the maker of our world. Additionally, we also recognize that our world exists as a present reality and not as a future possibility. And finally, by speaking the first two words of the code, we boldly proclaim that no one, including God, may lay claim to our sovereign domain.

After the first two words of the code establish the definitive owner of our world, the third word explains its function. We design our world to serve because that is how God designed His world. Everything in the World Maker's world seeks to serve in the survival, comfort, and orchestration of everyone else's world. The more we design our world toward a similar level of service, the more we'll find human creators, creation, and the Creator eager partners in our world-making effort.

Once the code establishes the maker and function of our world, it then outlines who our world serves. The first recipient for service is our soul. The creator's code demands that the supreme service of every world be given to its maker. As always, God's world is the model. For example, creation allows human beings to rule, fill, and subdue her, but only because doing so serves her Creator's intentions. Likewise, the first responsibility of our world is to serve our soul as its maker.

Before two world makers can partner together, each must present themselves as the only authority over their own unique world. Only after both established themselves as two separate sovereigns over two separate worlds should they begin exploring the possibility of an orchestrational partnership. Presently, every soul is either a world taker or a recovering world taker. Consequently, the creator's code exists to safeguard everyone from the long-established spiritual, inner, and material habits we've all formed after years of bearing the taker's likeness.

The soul who seeks to be the foremost authority in another's world is a taker. At the same time, the soul who willfully allows another soul to take their position as the foremost authority within their world is also a taker by feigning material submission so they might gain access to and, eventually, seize control over their invader's world. Consequently, the creator's code requires every sovereign soul to remain the one and only maker of their own unique world.

The code's second stipulation requires our world to also serve the intentions of all our material partners. The list of our material partners begins with creation and includes every human partner we've previously outlined: a spousal partner, intimate partners, familiar partners, regular partners, seen partners, and unseen partners. Living by the code requires us to design our world to serve the intentions of all. Such a challenging stipulation obligates us to continually seek to understand creation and our fellow human creators so our world might more ideally serve their survival, comfort, and orchestration.

Friction between creators, as well as between creators and creation, is unavoidable. The code does not exist to stop such inevitable unpleasantness. Instead, the code exists to use these unavoidable clashes to redirect humanity's world-taking efforts toward mutually beneficial world-making efforts.

We all want partners. As finite beings, we'll each require at least some assistance while orchestrating our unique world. Living by the code ensures that we don't lose sight of our earnest desire for orchestrational partners amidst the tensions that will arise amidst the contentious nature of human interactions.

Our partners get upset when we step on, don't understand, or outright ignore their world-making intentions. The code helps us glean the hidden value laden within such tense moments. Living by the code requires us to look past our offended partner's anger to see the opportunity being offered to improve the service our world offers to their world. Once we begin understanding, respecting, and championing the intentions of our world-making partners, then they'll likewise begin searching for creative ways to reciprocate.

The code's third stipulation requires our world to also serve the intentions of God. Our first step in serving God is to allow Him alone to rule, fill, and subdue every soul, free from our "well-intentioned" meddling. The billions of human beings not covered by the code's second stipulation are covered by the third. God wants every spiritual being exclusively under His spiritual authority. The World Maker will not take kindly to us trying to usurp His position over any sovereign being. Designing a world that serves God's intentions requires that we keep our soul and our world from taking, especially regarding those with whom we have no level of partnership, and, therefore, no direct reason to serve.

Our world further serves God's intentions by generously offering survival, comfort, and orchestrational value to all. God wants everyone growing as their own spiritual, inner, and material world maker. Once our world is globally engaged in the making of world makers, we'll find the World Maker far more invested in our orchestrational ambitions.

God desires to grow each into a world maker who is uniquely ruling, filling, and subduing their personal portion of Mother Nature into their own unique world while allowing and aiding everyone else to do likewise. However, these general intentions of God do not even scratch the surface of the Unknowable One's plans. God's knowledge, desires, and intentions remain infinitely incomprehensible. Still, the deeper we live in a timeless, spaceless, and matterless union with Him, the more our soul may take on His likeness, thereby enabling us to serve His broader aims. Therefore, living by the code obligates us to strive toward being with God in the present moment so that we might orchestrate our world toward more fully serving His timeless, spaceless, and matterless intentions.

The fourth and final stipulation in the creator's code is the unfortunate responsibility we bear as world makers still living amidst a fallen age. While the first three stipulations of the creator's code exist to aid everyone's world-making efforts, the fourth and final stipulation exists to obstruct everyone's world-taking efforts. Since no soul yet exists completely purged of the taker's likeness, the code's final stipulation is tragically essential until the end of the present age.

Fortunately, the creator's code does not require us to stop everyone who is attempting to be the One. Such a stipulation would certainly produce unending and pointless warfare. Instead, living by the code requires that we build our world in a way that obstructs world takers from fully actualizing their spiritual desire to rule, fill, and subdue the entirety of God's world and God's people.

A basic strategy for obstructing a world taker might be to punch them in the face the moment we sense their schemes to rule, fill, or subdue beyond their personal domain. However, exercising such a strategy would soon result in the breaking of every bone in both hands, not to mention the loss of all our personal freedoms. Instead, we must settle on a more elegant strategy by joining Mother Nature in forming deeply interwoven anatomical obstructions to every soul's desire to be like God—beginning with the most dangerous soul of all.

Our world is material. However, the enemy's likeness, which has tainted and corrupted every soul, is spiritual. Consequently, a material world cannot alter spiritual corruption. Even Mother Nature, who has spent millennia obstructing fallen beings, has yet to turn a single world taker into a world maker. Nonetheless, creation is quite adept at obstructing fallen beings from attaining a position of material divinity.

Creating a world to obstruct world takers starts by obstructing oneself, the most devious taker of all. Since our world is wrapped around a recovering world taker, the first and foremost insurgent requiring mitigation is us. The only way to truly ensure the safety of our world would be to permanently separate it from our soul. Since that is not a viable option, we'll need to make some concessions regarding the purity of our world amidst the present age. Like creation, we must willfully allow our world to endure enough corruption to expose our taking-tactics but not enough to instantaneously manifest death.

Despite our species being world takers, creation still allows us to rule, fill, and subdue her to a level of corruption that she deems acceptable. Our mother hopes her sacrificial service will help each mentally perceive, emotionally feel, and physically experience their foolish attempts to be like God. As a result, creation allows all to execute their taking-tactics until each has overreached in their efforts to be the One over everyone, at which point she pulls the anatomical rug out from beneath our soul so that we might fall into our void of infinite emptiness.

Mother Nature hopes her efforts toward obstructive exposure will cause enough suffering to compel each to spiritually return to Infinite Fullness before bodily death ensues. However, as a material partner, creation cannot force a spiritual being to surrender to her Creator. Our mother can expose our taking-tactics, but she must trust us to recognize our nature as takers so we might consensually bow before the Maker.

A world-making sovereign who lives by the creator's code will intentionally design their world to work with creation toward obstructively exposing all takers, starting with themselves. What we bring to our partnership with creation is our spiritual being. As a resurrected world-making authority, we, unlike Mother Nature, may lead takers to the Maker. Although we cannot make another soul surrender to God, we can obstruct them from materially consuming creation, expose their soul's void of infinite emptiness, and point them toward Infinite Fullness.

Like the World Maker's world, our world may also obstruct takers by helping all mentally perceive, emotionally feel, and physically experience their taking-tactics before bodily death ensues. Those not living by the creator's code will respond to the obstructive service of our world as they see fit. Those living by the creator's code will revere our world's obstructive service as vital to their continuing opportunity to orchestrate their world alongside our world amidst God's world.

While obstructing takers, we must remember that only their spiritual being bears the enemy's likeness. Damaging the mind, heart, or body of another accomplishes nothing. Even shaming a taker's thoughts, emotions, and actions is counterproductive. A champion of orchestration works toward ignoring all material forms of taking by focusing on the spiritual taker within. The Creator and creation will handle the consequences of material taking. Our job, as the Kingdom of Creators, is to obstruct each soul as a world taker and lead all to the World Maker.

Each human being's inner realm is an integral aspect of Mother Nature. Therefore, each mind, heart, and body respond favorably to a spiritual authority who is materially obstructing their tainted soul in a way that leads them away from world-taking and toward world-making. At the same time, no one's inner realm responds well to a spiritual authority who is condemning their mental, emotional, and physical efforts as evil. Each mind, heart, and body still operate rightfully under the assumption that, as integral aspects of creation, everything they produce is good. Therefore, condemning another's thoughts, emotions, and actions as evil will only serve to let their soul off the hook.

151

As the Kingdom of Creators, we're generous with a taker's mind, heart, and body, but not with their soul. We must surgically deal with the spiritual ringleader without unjustly punishing their material compatriots. Every mind, heart, and body still operates in obedience to God as they express their spiritual sinner with material sin. Punishing another's inner realm for elegantly expressing their sinful soul is counterproductive. After all, if a sovereign is going to orchestrate their own unique world within God's world of unique worlds, then they'll need their mind, heart, and body fully affirmed of their goodness. The Kingdom of Creators exists to populate God's world with a plethora of uniquely human worlds. Damaging the mind, heart, and body of a taker is a last resort, to only be utilized when an unrepentant soul has so thoroughly corrupted their inner realm that they're an unrelenting mental, emotional, and physical threat to every world and every world maker, requiring them to be permanently removed from God's world.

A belligerent soul is best dealt with by leading their mind, heart, and body toward world-making while simultaneously disciplining the taker within. As fallen souls, we each instinctively use our material humanity like a shield, because Mother Nature has always been, remains, and will always be good. Therefore, whenever we're caught in the act of taking, we simply uphold the good anatomical structures sheltering our sinful, rebellious, and evil soul. Once exposed as a replication of the world taker, we prefer punishment falling upon our mind, heart, and body, thereby allowing our soul to escape judgment. The moment an external disciplinary authority accuses our fleshly shield of evil, our sinful soul slips away scot-free as creation receives the punishment for our transgressions. Additionally, we then feel a perverse sense of delight at having duped an external authority into passing a profane and revisionist judgment upon God's good material realm.

As champions of orchestration, we discipline takers by first authentically praising their mind, heart, and body for good and faithful service. Only after a taker's mind, heart, and body feel genuinely appreciated will they step aside and allow us to deal with their tainted sovereign. As integral aspects of creation, each soul's inner realm of mind, heart, and body retains nurturing instincts that impel them to protect their soul from undue harm. Therefore, our first responsibility as a champion of orchestration is to win over a taker's material mind, heart, and body so we might deal with the tainted soul within.

Dealing with a spiritual taker does not require us to use thoughts, emotions, or actions since doing so would unnecessarily involve both inner realms in the disciplinary act. Instead, we discipline a taker by being a maker, an art we first experienced from the Maker as He laid siege to our soul. While God is besieging our souls, He's disciplining us regarding who we are, who He is, and who we could be together. Likewise, we discipline takers by simply being a living, growing, and unique world maker, who is authoritatively leading their mind, heart, and body toward ruling, filling, and subduing their own unique world within God's world.

While we're inspiring a taker's mind, heart, and body toward world-making, we're simultaneously disciplining the tainted soul within. A champion of orchestration tangibly demonstrates their world-making likeness by inspiring a taker's mind, enthralling a taker's heart, and empowering a taker's body toward making their own sovereign domain. Simply experiencing a world maker in action is devastating for one trying to pass themselves off as the World Maker. Still, each sovereign soul may respond to our spiritual discipline as they see fit. However, if we've already won over their mind, heart, and body, then we leave them with few options for thinking, feeling, and acting out their belligerence.

Spiritually being a creator is the essence of human authority. A world maker living by the creator's code designs their world to obstruct anyone attempting to be the One. Additionally, those living by the code will design their world to discipline world takers and lead them toward the World Maker. Then, each soul might make choose to join the Kingdom of Creators and live by the creator's code so they, too, might pursue the supreme aim of our species—making their world within the world of unique worlds that we exist to make for the World Maker.

We design our world to obstruct takers so we might lead all to the One capable of making everyone into a unique one. Still, as the Kingdom of Creators, we must honor the code while disciplining others. The temptation to seize control over a tainted soul, their chaotic inner realm, and their imploding material realm will be strong. After all, successfully obstructing, exposing, and disciplining anyone attempting to be the like One will make us look, feel, and act an awful lot like the One.

Living by the creator's code is the foundation for orchestrational partnerships within the Kingdom of Creators. Each soul must make a world that serves their intentions, their partners' intentions, and their Creator's intentions while obstructing anyone attempting to be the One. If we fail to live by the code, then there is no hope for any world-making partnerships amidst humanity. Although we may still manage to survive comfortably together without the code, no one will risk condemning their world to invasion by partnering with takers.

Without the creator's code, we'll all simply continue altering our taking-tactics so we might invade everyone's world and become the One who is ruling, filling, and subduing all worlds. As a result, no one will ever get around to orchestrating their own unique world as we all fight over who is the supreme subduer, filler, and ruler of God's world. Therefore, each soul living by the creator's code will obstruct world takers while building a coalition of world makers, so humanity, creation, and the Creator might return to orchestrating everyone's world amidst Mother Nature so she might become our world of unique worlds.

Chapter 20
Soul Identity

When a new material member of our species arrives, they receive a legal identity to distinguish them from the rest of humanity. When a new spiritual member of humanity arrives, they receive a soul identity to distinguish them from the rest of the world-making creators. With a legal identity and a soul identity in place, an individual is fully identifiable as a human, world-making being.

God does not impart a soul identity the way parents impart a legal identity. Our Heavenly Father speaks, shapes, and breathes His likeness directly into our soul to give birth to one who is unlike anyone, including Him. Then, our Maker trusts us to recognize the uniqueness He's endowed upon us by selecting our own soul identity.

Identifying our spiritual being requires considering how God identifies His spiritual Being. In this regard, God tells us that "I AM." God's name for Himself comes across as a bit perplexing until we remember that He exists outside of time, space, and matter. Therefore, as the spiritual Source for every material object, God chose a name to remind us that "I AM" is the spiritual Source for whatever material object we happen to be considering at the time. So, as we see, feel, and experience something in creation, all we need to do is place "I AM" before the thing to get a glimpse into God's infinite identity. For example, Mother Nature's material approximations of light, love, and life exist to entice us closer to the spiritual Creator so He might reveal to our soul that "I AM Light, Love, and Life."

Recognizing God's method for identifying Himself as the eternal, boundless, and infinite, "I AM" is the foundation for our soul identity. Spiritually walking alongside the "I AM" naturally results in our soul growing into an "I am." The moment we surrender unconditionally to God, the vacuous spiritual womb within our soul is inseminated, giving birth to a living spiritual being who, for the first time, may say, "I am." Then, the word we choose to place after "I am" is our soul identity.

Unlike the "I AM," we're not the spiritual Source for every material thing. Instead, we must pick just one attribute from our Creator as our "I am." This singular attribute is our personal form of spiritual identification, which God has designed us to personify in the spiritual realm so that we might give that likeness into our inner realm so our mind, heart, and body might do likewise into creation's material realm. An example of a soul identity is the pen name used to identify the author of this book, which, of course, is not a pen name but a soul identity.

We do not pick our soul identity out of a hat, although God's hat would indeed be quite large. Instead, we each must allow God to speak, touch, and breathe His likeness into our soul so that we might be spiritually born into the unique one we desire to become and our Beloved desires to make. Then, as we ponder God's spiritual craftsmanship of our unique being, we may decide which one of His infinite attributes we now uniquely personify so we might claim that attribute as our soul identity.

God is indivisible. As our soul unites with Him, we get all of His Infinite Fullness amidst each and every moment of our timeless faith. However, like the rest of finite material creation bound within time, space, and matter, no one human being gets to express every attribute of the Unknowable One. Instead, everyone must recognize the one attribute the Maker is custom crafting their soul to personify.

Mother Nature sublimely models how the finite might express the Infinite. After all, she is the holistic material approximation of the spiritual One. In the pursuit of her expressive charge, creation strives to keep each one of her countless anatomical wonders expressing only one attribute of the Infinite One. Similar to how a rock expresses Strength, a flower expresses Beauty, and an ocean expresses Depth, so every aspect of creation tends toward expressing one attribute of the Infinite One. As unique human creators, we each exercise a different perspective on which trait is most predominately expressed by creation's rocks, flowers, and oceans. However, we all still tend toward honoring creation's intent for each one of her anatomical treasures to gloriously display just one attribute of her Beloved. Therefore, a sovereign soul honors our material mother's expressive model by selecting only one attribute of their Creator as their soul identity.

Those who avoid picking a soul identity do so to keep their spiritual being unknowable. As fallen beings, we each desire to retain the possibility that we might be, or might be on the verge of becoming, the Unknowable One. After all, the Creator did come as a human being. As a result, all fallen souls desire to maintain the mystery that they might be the One, to give themselves sufficient time to make themselves into the One. However, the moment a human being selects a singular attribute of the Creator as their soul identity, they eliminate their chance of being recognized as "I AM."

Despite dispelling our chance at divinity, the benefits of selecting a singular soul identity are significant across all three realms. First, identifying and embracing God's craftsmanship within our soul pleases our Creator. Additionally, embracing the foremost attribute that our Maker is spiritually endowing upon our soul will further arouse God for an even deeper spiritual union with us. Then, the more passionate our spiritual union with the Creator becomes, the more profoundly God will endow us with the attribute that we most delight in personifying.

Our inner realm will also respond well to a singular soul identity. Forming profound thoughts, potent emotions, and powerful actions for a soul devoid of an identity is rather difficult. However, giving our mind, heart, and body a single attribute to express—although still immensely challenging—at least gives them some source material to work with.

Creation also favors a soul with a singular identity. Since our mother expresses every attribute of our Father, she gets rather offended when we try to present ourselves as a better version of God, which she rightly fears will also result in a parallel attempt to replace her. Selecting only one attribute of God to identify our soul is a strong indication to creation that we do not desire to replace her or her Creator. Instead, selecting a singular attribute of God as our soul identity is how we express our desire to creation for her assistance in materially displaying the one attribute of her Creator that we uniquely personify, something we'll find her both eager and able to achieve.

Each soul's union with God is unique. Although we each live with the same Source, God's infinite nature provides everyone with the means for spiritual distinction. However, God's spiritual realm is not a divine buffet. We each innately understand that only one can be the One, which is why we're all scrambling to be that One. God's infinite attributes are what make Him, and Him alone, the One and only Source that everyone must draw upon to receive their own soul identity.

A common misconception within our present age is to claim that everyone's god is God. In fact, a more accurate conclusion would be to say that everyone's god is not God. After all, as fallen souls, we construct a god in our likeness in a doomed attempt to present ourselves as God. Similar to how God originally made us in His likeness, we, as fallen creators, have the perverse temerity to attempt to make a god in our likeness. For example, fallen souls who identify God as loving tend to be loving, fallen souls who identify God as judgmental tend to be judgmental, and fallen souls who identify God as aloof from the concerns of humanity tend to be aloof from the concerns of humanity. Even those who live with the Unknowable One will never fully know the

Unknowable One. The best we can do is identify the one attribute of God that we uniquely personify. Fully identifying the Infinite One is simply not an option for finite beings.

Like the process of selecting a child's legal identity, the process involved in selecting one's soul identity takes time. It is not abnormal for parents to spend years exploring names before even conceiving a child. Once conception does take place, parents will then use the ensuing months to continue the naming discussion. Sometimes, the child's name will remain undecided until seeing the infant. Other times, further delays will transpire that will withhold the child's name until long after birth. However, a name is always found because one who materially exists must be distinguished from those who already materially exist, a principle that also holds true in the spiritual realm.

Identifying the foremost attribute that God is speaking, touching, and breathing into our soul takes time. Although God's work is spiritual and timeless, the tangible name we select to identify His craftsmanship is material. As parents will attest, the moment the name for their child arrives, they, and everyone around them, will immediately acknowledge the inseparable nature between the new being and the name identifying the new being. Similarly, the moment we discover the one attribute that we personally personify as a unique spiritual being, we'll be able to tell others that, "I am...". Identifying our soul is a rite of passage within the Kingdom of Creators that allows each world maker to distinguish themselves as one who wishes to not only be known as a human but also as an independent, sovereign, and unique world-making being.

The more words the less meaning. Therefore, our soul identity holds the most meaning when we use only one word. Finding the one word that materially encapsulates the entirety of our spiritual being is a daunting undertaking. Fortunately, our mother is eager to assist us in identifying the spiritual craftsmanship of our Father.

All our lives, we've been materially chasing our soul identity. At the core of all our past sinful efforts was the attempt to take our spiritual identity from material creation. Should we intently ponder our taking-tactics, we'll find a single word that summarizes the supreme aim of what we'd hoped to achieve. We were not merely trying to get something. We were trying to become someone. Our mother allowed our foolishness so that, once we surrendered to our Father, we'd have the perceptions, sensations, and experiences required to aid us in discovering the soul identity we tried to take from her and have finally received from God.

A soul identity also helps us cultivate human partners. A name is a container for meaning. Our legal identity helps humanity categorize our ethnicity, culture, sex, legal status, time period, lineage, and many other elements important to human society. Our soul identity helps creators categorize our being, relation to God, orchestrational intentions, service to the world, submission to the code, and many other elements important to the Kingdom. We use our legal identity when interacting with humanity. We use our soul identity when interacting with creators.

Every orchestrational partner wants to know which unique attribute of God their world will receive from us. Likewise, we want to know which unique attribute of God our world will receive from each of our orchestrational partners. The soul who does not spiritually identify themselves will make other world makers nervous. After all, any spiritual being without a singular identity is still trying to be the Identity.

No one wants anyone else to identify their soul. Each sovereign is personally responsible for identifying the Creator's craftsmanship of their spiritual being. Selecting a soul identity is for those determined to communicate that they are no longer merely human but also a unique spiritual being. Then, as every member of the Kingdom of Creators lives out their soul identity, we will, together, form one grand orchestrational tapestry that gloriously and uniquely portrays "I AM."

Chapter 21
The Three Orders

God's hostile takeover of His family business reveals how dedicated He remains to His goal of growing a race of unique world makers who will rule, fill, and subdue Mother Nature into a world of unique worlds. The Great Imperative, which echoes through the Greatest Commandment and Great Commission, further confirms God's desire for every soul to grow into a sovereign world maker amidst the present fallen age, as well as in the age of creators yet to come. Therefore, as the Kingdom of Creators, we honor God's commitment to the Great Imperative by permanently decentralizing our authority by dividing ourselves into three independent, interconnected, and interdependent orders: the Ruling Order, the Filling Order, and the Subduing Order.

Human beings create governmental, religious, cultural, financial, social, and a plethora of other institutions to ensure the comfortable survival of all. As world makers, we institute the three orders to ensure the orchestrational success of all. One of the main problems inherent to us individually fulfilling the Great Imperative is that we're finite. Therefore, the three orders are designed to enable the Kingdom of Creators to share the load of the Great Imperative by inspiring every world maker to live as a ruler, a filler, or a subduer.

One of the first curiosities a tainted soul will sense when considering the three orders is whether the possibility exists of joining and mastering all three. However, there is only One who is the Ruler, the Filler, and the Subduer. Only a soul bearing the likeness of God's enemy seeks to be the Triune Master. As a result, committing to only one of the three orders is a vital check against each soul's desire to be like God.

Selecting the order that we wish to join from among the three is a simple matter. After all, everyone is either a foremost thinker, feeler, or doer. Although we all create thoughts, emotions, and actions, we each display a notable expertise in only one of the three. Committing to mastering the one inner creative realm where we hold a natural talent will also significantly increase the orchestrational value we offer to others. Once we're engaged in the orchestration of our own unique world, it will grow rapidly apparent how invaluable it is to be surrounded by those wielding their own mental, emotional, or physical expertise.

Our personal creative expertise is where we all return when things get rough. Amidst life's challenges, some take time to think, others step back to feel through the issues, and yet more get to doing something until a resolution presents itself. Our personal realm of creative expertise is the springboard we all use to problem-solve, innovate, and sustain our world-making efforts.

We acknowledge our creative expertise by joining either the Ruling Order of thinkers, the Filling Order of feelers, or the Subduing Order of doers. Making such a choice provides us with significant benefits. First, we join those who are committed to living their life in the likeness of the Ruling Father, the Filling Spirit, and the Subduing Son. Second, we highlight our personal creative expertise, which immediately communicates to others how we might supplement their creative limitations. Third, we gain access to expert thinkers, feelers, and doers, who are each seeking mutually beneficial partnerships that will lead toward the orchestration of their unique world alongside everyone else's unique world, so all bring forth a world of unique worlds.

A simpler way to understand the three orders is to view them through the character that each personifies. The Subduing Son is the Warrior, the Filling Spirit is the Wizard, and the Ruling Father is the Will. Consequently, we join one of the Kingdom's three orders based upon our personal creative expertise so we might live our life as a subduing warrior, a filling wizard, or a ruling will. Then, we may live out our own narrative revelation of how we experience the member of the Godhead that we wish to uniquely personify.

Every story throughout human history drew its characters from the Trinity. We all want to see, feel, and experience how warriors, wizards, and wills work together as a creative team. The more provocative a storyteller makes the three original characters, the more engrossing the story. An epic storyteller crafts numerous characterizations of each member of the Trinity and then shows how they all work together to achieve an otherwise impossible and mutually beneficial end. We all enjoy stories portraying how warriors, wizards, and wills work together because that is how the Trinity works, and that is also how we're supposed to work as God's race of unique world makers.

As the Kingdom of Creators, we lead humanity's orchestrational efforts by living as a vast host of determined warriors, defiant wizards, and dedicated wills who are leading all toward orchestrating everyone's world amidst God's world. Mankind will follow such inspiring figures because each sovereign soul yearns to be a character of narrative distinction amidst a noble cast. Every single human being is already striving to live out their own particular likeness of the Warrior, the Wizard, or the Will. The reason we're all struggling is that we're not spiritually living with the Warrior, the Wizard, and the Will.

The three orders are also a vital check against everyone's desire to rule, fill, and subdue all. As we've seen throughout human history, whenever rulers get out of hand, the warriors are sent in to subdue them. Similarly, whenever warriors get out of hand, it's the wizards who create a technological wonder nullifying their battlefield prowess. At other times, wizards get too powerful, requiring rulers to pass laws banning their dangerous practices. Living together as warriors, wizards, and wills creates a rock-paper-scissors-like check against each tainted soul's lingering desire to be like God.

No soul is the Warrior, the Wizard, or the Will which is why each of the Kingdom's three orders will remain forever devoid of a singular, top-down hierarchical leader. Instead, each soul living within one of the Kingdom's three orders will remain exclusively under their own authority so they might live out their own unique characterization of the one member of the triune Godhead that they desire to uniquely portray. At the same time, the moment any soul attempts to usurp the sovereign authority of another the order that naturally counters their creative expertise will send in the appropriate subduers, fillers, or rulers to obstructively expose their desire to rule, fill, and subdue all. Therefore, the Kingdom's three orders exist to wholly decentralize human authority all the way down to each and every soul so that every single sovereign might remain the maker of their world and the taker of none.

The Trinity charged us with three tasks and gave us three characters based upon the three members of the Trinity to achieve this triune end. As finite beings, we share the load of the Great Imperative by encouraging every creator to focus on their creative expertise as a thinking will, a feeling wizard, or a doing warrior. Then, as each sovereign soul remains focused on their creative strength, the Kingdom of Creators will provide humanity with the determined warriors, defiant wizards, and determined wills needed to assist everyone toward ruling, filling, and subduing their own unique world, alongside everyone else's unique world, so that we all might bring forth a world of unique worlds.

Every creator needs ruling thoughts, filling emotions, and subduing actions. Lacking even one of these inner creative domains is disastrous for world-making. As finite beings living within the limitations of time, space, and matter, no one will ever personally possess the mental, emotional, and physical mastery needed to orchestrate their own unique world. However, focusing on developing our personal creative expertise, while partnering with others who are doing likewise, gives us the hope of transacting our creative expertise with others, so all might acquire a sufficiency of ruling thoughts, filling emotions, and subduing actions for their world.

An example of submitting to the three orders is this book, which is designed to fill its reader with clarity. The soul identity we select defines our spiritual being, while the order we select defines our material character. God is the original triune character. His three persons of the Subduing Warrior, the Filling Wizard, and the Ruling Will remain the only three characters available for our species to embody. Although we cannot personally emulate all three members of the Trinity, joining one of the three orders makes us a member of a larger community, which, as a whole, portrays a unique, united, and growing personification of the triune Godhead.

The Warrior, the Wizard, and the Will already exist in the spiritual realm. However, creation yearns for the opportunity to create a grand interconnected stage for us as God's race of unique warriors, wizards, and wills. Our soul's job is to spiritually live with the Trinity so we might know the Warrior, the Wizard, and the Will. Then, we may live out our life as a unique warrior within the Subduing Order, a unique wizard within the Filling Order, or a unique will within the Ruling Order.

God designed humanity to subdue, fill, and rule Mother Nature as determined warriors, defiant wizards, and dedicated wills. The soul who expresses their soul identity through one of God's three persons will always remain relevant. Just as stories about warriors, wizards, and wills never go out of style, so a soul who lives their life as one of the original triune characters will never lack for an audience.

Living as a unique warrior, wizard, or will is exciting. However, living amongst a noble cast of unique warriors, wizards, and wills is epic.

As creators, we cultivate partnerships with one another by committing to the creator's code, selecting our own soul identity, and living together as the subduing warriors, the filling wizards, and the ruling wills of creation. The three orders exist to obstruct everyone from world-taking while also ensuring everyone is growing together toward the life of epic world-making adventure that we all crave.

The grand narratives that have timelessly inspired mankind have always been an articulation of how culturally relevant warriors, wizards, and wills have worked together amidst their ancient codes, identities, and orders to achieve otherwise impossible ends. The church is God's intended location to cultivate that very narrative into actual reality. As the Kingdom of Creators who operate as the caretakers of the Great Imperative, we are the champions of orchestration empowered by our individual and intimate union with the Trinity to live together—and make worlds together—as the foremost warriors, wizards, and wills of our age.

Section 8
Cultivating Creators

The Kingdom of Creators partners with the Creator and creation by inspirationally leading mankind back toward being a race of unique world makers who are making Mother Nature into our world of unique worlds. First, the Kingdom of Creators guides each soul toward orchestrating their own unique world through the life-long plan of the seven uniques. Then, the Kingdom of Creators directs each world maker toward serving the Creator, creation, and every other human creator by joining one of the Kingdom's seven battalions so they might assist in the survival, comfort, and orchestration of all. Finally, the Kingdom of Creators inspires all sovereign souls to design their most significant human partnership toward uniquely portraying the first partnership, where the Masculine Creator and the feminine creation originally united to bring forth the first unique world.

Chapter 22
The Seven Uniques

Those who intend to create their own unique world must follow the original model. Curiously, God orchestrated His world across seven days, even though His infinite orchestrational capacity did not require a segmented effort. The principal purpose for God's world is to grow unique world makers. Therefore, even the seven-step process He used while making His world was intentionally designed to assist each world maker in making their world. As a result, each unique one must likewise create their world by using a seven-step process to align their orchestrational effort with God's original world-making template.

Fortunately, we do not need to recreate anything God has already created. Human beings cannot create from the void. Instead, we are the void from which God spiritually creates and we materially express. As growing world makers, we intentionally reorchestrate anatomical matter into the material forms we require to approximate the spiritual being that God has already brought forth from within our soul.

The Infinite One created His world in seven days. As finite beings, we must approach our orchestration effort realistically. Instead of trying to create our world in seven days, we must orchestrate our world across the course of a lifetime through the seven uniques. The seven uniques, once fully achieved, will culminate in every human being's highest material aspiration, the orchestration of their own unique world.

We create the seven uniques in the following order: a unique body, a unique skill, a unique enterprise, a unique family, a unique team, a unique position, and a unique legacy. As the Creator's model of the seven days reveals, each orchestrational act builds upon the previous so that the resulting whole might serve its creator's principal purpose. God's principal purpose is to grow unique world makers, and everything about His world serves this singular end. Likewise, our unique world must serve our principal purpose that we spiritually embody, inwardly form, and materially express.

Up until this point, we've left the definition of a unique world intentionally vague. The reason being the seven uniques are what define a uniquely human world. Consequently, when a human being spends their life making their own unique body, skill, enterprise, family, team, position, and legacy, the result is their own unique world.

Pursuing our first unique requires repurposing the personal flesh endowed upon our soul so we might turn it into a customized mental, emotional, and physical vessel of orchestrational power. After achieving our unique body, we'll naturally progress toward orchestrating our unique skill. Then, our unique skill will lead us toward our unique enterprise. As a result, our unique enterprise will subsequently provide the means for our unique family. Afterward, our unique family will establish the foundation for our unique team. And our unique team will then work to place us into a unique position of orchestrational significance. Lastly, existing in our own unique position of orchestrational significance will enable us to leave a unique and lasting legacy on the earth.

A common misconception when looking over the seven uniques is to consider that we've already achieved a few. After all, we all have a body and at least a few skills. Additionally, all human beings are enterprising and have some sort of family. However, these basic elements of our existence are not unique; they're personal. Due to our Father's wishes, our mother has worked diligently to provide each soul with a personalized body, skill, enterprise, family, team, position, and rapidly approaching legacy. She cannot make anything unique for us, but she can surround each potential world maker with the raw resources necessary for them to begin making their own unique world.

Turning our personal body into a unique body is the first step. Creating a unique body requires pursuing a specific achievement within a realistic timeframe that culminates in the acquisition of a title for our newly orchestrated flesh. Even more importantly, the achievement, timeframe, and title we select for our first unique must align with our principal purpose. Putting on thirty pounds of muscle, running a marathon, or losing fifteen pounds are all potentially desirable achievements. However, if none of those desirable achievements shape our body into the form we need to mentally, emotionally, and physically fulfill our principal purpose, then we've failed to orchestrate a unique body capable of orchestrating our unique world.

We choose an achievement for our first unique that will reshape our physical form into a customized vessel for achieving our principal purpose. Short-term benefits such as being more attractive, healthy, or energetic are all secondary considerations. The most important consideration for our unique body is what we need our body to think, feel, and do so that we might leave a unique and lasting legacy that will fulfill our principal purpose across the span of generations.

The seven uniques help world makers focus on the long game. The World Maker created His world with an unerring focus on His principal purpose. Likewise, our unique body, skill, enterprise, family, team, position, and legacy must all serve in the achievement of our supreme aim. What that aim is, arrives through God's spiritual craftsmanship, our inward interpretation of God's craftsmanship, and creation's aid in materially approximating the principal purpose we bear.

We have seven uniques to achieve across the remainder of our days. The time frame we select for completing each unique will likely vary from a few months to a few decades. As spiritual beings, we honor creation by learning how to fulfill our world-making intentions inside her finite realm of time, space, and matter. Therefore, each of our seven uniques must be attached to an estimated time frame to help us, other human creators, creation, and the Creator plan accordingly. Furthermore, the seven uniques are more than a personal planning tool. The seven uniques are also a blueprint that will help us communicate effectively and efficiently with each of our world-making partners.

After choosing an achievement and a timeframe for each unique, we must then select a title to impart upon the completion of each unique. A title formally recognizes what we've brought forth as a living entity. As parents name each child that they bring into God's world, a creator must name each unique they bring into their world.

As world makers, we alone impart living status to the seven uniques comprising our world. After all, a world that is not alive is not a world. Therefore, each world looks to its maker for the recognition of its existence, its goodness, and its purpose. Consequently, if we treat our world as a non-living entity, then it will respond accordingly. However, if we treat our world as a living entity, then it will strive to live up to the inspiring titles that we, as its maker, endow.

After completing our unique body, we'll naturally begin pining to make our own unique skill. Unfortunately, all skills that presently exist are disqualified for consideration as our second unique. Instead, we must use the mind, heart, and body we've already aligned to our principal purpose to develop a previously non-existent skill. A world maker's unique skill is the one orchestrational capability that is so vital to their principal purpose that it cannot be entrusted to any other. Honing a unique skill is what allows our unique body to operate as the central orchestrational engine for our lifelong, world-making effort.

Like orchestrating a unique body, orchestrating a unique skill requires pursuing a specific achievement within a realistic time frame to acquire a personally endowed title. It's also important to note how each successive unique gets more demanding. Orchestrating a unique body from the human flesh that we already have is challenging but doable while orchestrating a unique skill that does not yet exist is far more difficult. However, having a unique body already aligned to and serving our principal purpose enables us to mentally, emotionally, and physically bring forth our second unique.

The seven uniques, like the seven days, are designed to instill orchestrational momentum across the span of a lifetime. Each day of God's seven days led elegantly to the next. Likewise, each of the seven uniques we complete will propel us forward toward the culmination of our world and the principal purpose it will fulfill.

Orchestrating a unique skill will prepare us to progress to our third unique. A unique enterprise is the structure we erect around our unique body to enable the effective and efficient delivery of our unique skill to all. Commerce will likely be involved in our unique enterprise, but for a world maker, the exchange of currency will remain ancillary. A world maker measures their value by how effectively they're giving to all what they have already received from God, and not the amount of the material reciprocation they receive for what they've given.

Successfully bringing forth a unique enterprise will provide a world maker with the time, freedom, and resources required to orchestrate their own unique family. We begin our fourth unique by taking stock of the personal elements of a family that Mother Nature has already provided and, if possible, reshape them into a unique family. A unique family is a committed core of creators who are orchestrating their own tightly-knit world of unique worlds. A world maker builds a microcosm of God's world of unique worlds within their unique family so that everyone within their family might make their own unique world—together—in a way no one individual could achieve without the assistance of everyone else, thereby preparing each to do likewise, on a larger scale, as they progress beyond their fourth unique.

Pursuing our fourth unique requires that we already have a robust body, a recognized skill, and an exciting enterprise to entice the family members that creation has already provided, and whoever else we might select to undergo the rigors of becoming a unique family. Orchestrating a unique family requires everyone to exercise the Great Commission upon everyone else so each might disciple, baptize, and teach all how to be indispensable partners for their world.

Orchestrating our fourth unique is, by design, the first time we should allow other creators into our fledgling realm. During our first three uniques, our world remains far too fragile for deep interaction with multiple sovereigns. Until we're pursuing the orchestration of a unique family, we should strive to keep our world isolated from the authoritative touch of others.

After thoroughly discipling, baptizing, and teaching each of our family members how to be part of a unique family, we're then ready to move on to our fifth unique of orchestrating a unique team. Partnering with the highly skilled and highly specialized creators needed to orchestrate our world requires exercising the Great Commission upon each. A few members of our unique team may be a part of our unique family, but most will not. The difference is that we make a place for our family members regardless of their orchestrational skills, while we make a place for our team members only because of their orchestrational skills.

Each member of our creative team will require customized access to our world so that they might apply their unique skills in a way that will ideally serve our principal purpose. Unfortunately, no other world maker, or their world, will come to us ready for partnership. Therefore, our fifth unique requires that we reorchestrate a portion of our world to elegantly integrate with each member of our unique team. Although such customized and detailed orchestrational craftsmanship on our world is laborious, it is also essential if we intend to progress.

Inside a unique team, every world maker serves in the fulfillment of every other world maker's principal purpose. No one inside a unique team sacrifices for the greater good. Instead, everyone inside a unique team fulfills their principal purpose in a way that will synchronously, simultaneously, and equally fulfill everyone else's principal purpose. God's world of unique worlds demands that no world maker surrender or even compromise their personal world-making intentions. Then, each may have their own unique world within His world of unique worlds.

After orchestrating a unique team, we'll have the skilled individuals around us required to build a unique position suitable to our unique body, skill, enterprise, and family. Fallen souls fight over pre-existing position of significance in the hope that occupying one will make them significant. However, a unique world maker does not require or even desire, a pre-existing position. Once a soul is living beneath the touch of Significance, they're already being touched, shaped, and breathed into their own unique likeness of Significance. Therefore, each world maker will design their own unique position of orchestrational significance so that they might effectively and efficiently wield their unique body, skill, enterprise, family, and team to the benefit of all.

Creating a unique and never-before-seen position in the material realm—customized to our spiritual likeness of Significance—is what allows a spiritual sovereign to rule, fill, and subdue a portion of material creation toward leaving a lasting legacy. However, a world maker's legacy will not last unless their principal purpose also serves the World Maker's principal purpose. If a sovereign soul cannot explain to creation how their legacy will help her grow a race of unique world makers to make her into a world of unique worlds, then Mother Nature will rapidly recycle their world back into the forms first orchestrated by God.

Nothing lasts in creation that does not serve in the fulfillment of the Creator's principal purpose. Mother Nature's atoms will always revert to their original state of goodness because creation knows that the forms that she held at the end of the seven days did serve in the fulfillment of her Creator's principal purpose, while everything humanity has brought forth since the first seventh day remains suspect in her eyes. Still, if a world maker boldly establishes their legacy as a service to our Father's race of unique world makers and our mother's world of unique worlds, then they may give creation pause enough to temporarily delay decay. Although nothing we bring forth will last forever, amidst the presently cursed, corrupted, and condemned age, the more efficiently and more effectively our principal purpose serves the Creator's principal purpose, the longer creation will sustain our world beyond bodily death.

Although a unique legacy is the seventh and final unique a world maker brings forth, it is the first decision they make. The first six uniques serve the seventh. Consequently, a unique legacy is a world maker's lasting embodiment of their principal purpose left to assist all toward becoming a race of unique world makers who, together, are bringing forth a world of unique worlds. Just as the World Maker rested on the seventh day so that He might delight in His world as good, so a world maker must rest their body at the completion of their seventh unique, so they also might delight in their world as good.

Although a world maker does not need to know the details of their end before they begin, they do need a spiritual inkling of the legacy they wish to leave. A world maker custom designs their unique body, skill, enterprise, family, team, position, and legacy to fulfill their principal purpose. Although we do not necessarily need our principal purpose in a succinct expression of words, we do need to personify it as a living spiritual being. Then, as a unique one personifying our own unique principal purpose, we may orchestrate our own unique world to leave our own unique and lasting legacy that will serve every world and every world maker within God's world of unique worlds.

Chapter 23
The Seven Battalions

The Kingdom of Creators fields seven battalions: the health battalion, the education battalion, the business battalion, the religion battalion, the media battalion, the government battalion, and the history battalion. Taken as a whole, the seven battalions comprise the seven pillars upholding human society. Those most responsible for sustaining and innovating these seven pillars will, and do, lead the species. Consequently, if a world maker intends to orchestrate a lasting world, then ensuring their life's work is integrated into one of the seven pillars that uphold human society will significantly increase the odds that their legacy will last. Therefore, the Kingdom of Creators encourages each world maker to join just one of the seven battalions so that they might orchestrate their world in a way that enables the survival, comfort, and orchestrational success of all.

Membership in a battalion requires a world maker to already have achieved at least their first two uniques. A committed creator is one with a unique body capable of exercising a unique skill. Until a soul is working on their unique enterprise, they simply don't have anything distinctive to offer a battalion's service to humanity.

As a world maker, we naturally desire to partner with the experts who are already working on the pillar of society where we intend to leave our legacy. Therefore, each of the Kingdom's seven battalions is a fertile field for committed creators where each world maker might bring forth their world in a way that serves every other world and every other world maker within God's world of unique worlds. Furthermore, working intimately alongside other aligned sovereign beings will ensure that our legacy is not only integrated meaningfully into human society but also into the lives of our most indispensable partners. Even more importantly, splintering all committed creators across the Kingdom's seven battalions will further obstruct everyone from getting into a position of authority over anyone. Diversified specialization is always a formidable obstacle to singular domination.

The Kingdom's seven battalions are designed to keep all world makers focused on serving humanity. Often in the past, the church has grown inwardly focused. Consequently, establishing the seven battalions as the supreme arena for world makers within the Kingdom of Creators inspires each sovereign soul to make their unique world in a manner that will serve every world within God's world. Additionally, the seven battalions exist to assist each growing world maker, which is why the seven battalions mirror the seven uniques.

A newly arrived spiritual being determined to orchestrate a unique body will find assistance from the creative experts within the health battalion. As the growing creator progresses toward their second unique, the education battalion will certainly have much to offer regarding the orchestration of their own unique skill. Moving down the list, we can see the parallel nature between the two sevens as each sovereign's unique enterprise is served by the business battalion, each sovereign's unique family is served by the religion battalion, each sovereign's unique team is served by the media battalion, each sovereign's unique position is served by the government battalion, and each sovereign's unique legacy is served by the history battalion. Although each world maker will join only one battalion, every sovereign pursuing the orchestration of their own unique world will be served by all seven.

Leading humanity in health, education, business, religion, media, government, and history requires bringing together the creative experts who share a personal commitment to each pillar of society. However, a world maker's personal passion for building a world that serves all worlds arises only after they've committed to orchestrating their own unique world. Therefore, the seven uniques are the prerequisites bringing each world maker to one of the seven battalions. We all want to leave a lasting legacy. The seven uniques are the blueprint assisting each to design their own life-long, orchestrational plan. The seven battalions are the gathering point where each might execute their world-making plan in a way that serves the survival, comfort, and orchestrational success of all.

The moment we begin planning out our seven uniques, it will immediately grow apparent how much assistance we'll require in bringing forth all seven components of our world. Consequently, joining a group of committed creators already working on the pillar of society where we intend to leave our legacy is the ideal environment for our orchestrational success. An example of the seven battalions in action is this book which is intentionally designed to fill its readers with clarity regarding religion.

The Kingdom's seven battalions exist to inspire each mature world-making creator toward uniquely serving humanity's health, education, business, religion, media, government, or history so that all might lead our species toward making a world of unique worlds. Fallen souls seek leadership to take power, prestige, or property from as many as possible, while resurrected souls seek leadership to make power, prestige, and property for as many as possible. The Kingdom's seven battalions exist to direct every believer's personal passion for orchestrating their unique world toward serving all worlds and all world makers within God's world of unique worlds.

The Kingdom of Creators is designed to elevate Christianity back into a leadership role within society. Currently, our species is rightfully resistant to the church reacquiring any type of influence within society. In the past, the church misused its position to take people and make them into Christians. However, human beings do not want leaders who tyrannically oppress them or their world into servility and conformity.

What human beings want are inspirational leaders who actively serve their survival, their comfort, and their orchestration so that they might make the world that only they can make for the world of unique worlds.

God creates the spiritual church of resurrected souls. Then, we use our minds, hearts, and bodies to create the material forms that will express God's spiritual church amidst our present age. Many past material forms of God's spiritual church have led to embarrassing ends. However, the imperfect material forms of the church do not diminish the spiritual majesty of God's eternal host of resurrected souls. Today, as the materially present members of God's church, we must consider but not concede to the previous material forms of Christendom. Then, we may take it upon ourselves to decide what material forms will best contextualize the splendor of God's spiritual church for our present age.

The Kingdom of Creators is one material form expressing God's spiritual church, specifically designed to ensure that no one gets into a position of authority over anyone—especially the one who made the Kingdom of Creators. Still, the Kingdom of Creators is not the only material form available for expressing God's spiritual church. The Kingdom of Creators is merely for those who value a decentralized form of Christendom, focused on cultivating creators, not Christians. Consequently, the Kingdom of Creators does not exist to take people and make them into institutionalized and indoctrinated followers. Instead, the Kingdom of Creators exists to obstruct world takers and lead each toward the One who might make them into their own, unique world maker. Then, each who consensually receives the World Maker's touch may begin touching Mother Nature to make their own unique world in a way that will assist all toward making a world of unique worlds.

Although the Kingdom of Creators is not a traditional religious institution, the same Christian foundation remains. Simply put, the only way to become a world-making creator is to live with the world-making

Creator. The Kingdom of Creators merely champions that the essence of being human is being a world maker, and the essence of being a world maker is to walk presently, intimately, and eternally with the World Maker. The Kingdom's seven battalions exist to inspire each sovereign toward making their world in a way that serves all, so mankind might remember that we are the race of unique world makers who are the only ones capable of making God's world into a world of unique worlds.

If we consider the Man's time upon the earth through the lens of the seven battalions, we'll get a striking insight into His style of leadership. While walking among us, the Man imparted health, educational instruction, financial advice, religious reform, media headlines, respect for governmental authority, and an endless stream of relevant historical considerations for modern issues. God is the Leader of our species. Consequently, those who live spiritually with the Leader will lead humanity in health, education, business, religion, media, government, and history. Any soul spiritually living with the Leader will materially live as a leader.

Unlike God, we remain finite beings. Therefore, instead of trying to personally lead mankind in all seven pillars of human society, as many dictators have tried, we must each join only the one battalion where we intend to leave our legacy. Joining only one battalion places us inside a core of committed creators who are working together to provide unparalleled survival, comfort, and orchestrational success for all. Additionally, achieving our final four uniques is extremely difficult without being surrounded by, and building partnerships with, other world-making creators. As a result, the Kingdom's seven battalions exist to bring committed creators together so that each might more effectively and more efficiently orchestrate their world toward serving every world, and every world maker, amidst God's world.

Chapter 24
The First Partnership

If we intend to create a world, then we should seriously consider forming a partnership for our world similar to the partnership responsible for creating the world. The first partnership brought together the One Masculine Creator and the original feminine creation who united to bring forth a race of unique world makers who would make a world of unique worlds. Unsurprisingly, the final act of the first partnership was to bring forth two material bodies, one to portray the Masculine Creator and the second to portray feminine creation. As a result, when two souls bring together one masculine body and one feminine body, then they, too, may form their own world-making partnership in the likeness of the first world-making partnership.

God did not create marriage. God created the male and female bodies. We created marriage, the vows, the legal contract, the social customs, the unspoken expectations, the concept of divorce, the manifold abuses, and the endless carnage of shattered lives left in the wake of every fallen union. Every element of relationships, other than the male and female bodies, is on us. Although we must not attempt to structurally change our masculine and feminine forms, everything else of human manufacture remains open to alteration. Once our souls look out through a creator's perspective, doctrines, and Kingdom then we may begin to understand what God intended when originally providing humanity with one masculine body and one feminine body.

As recovering world takers, the dangers inherent amidst a spousal union are manifold. Giving another fallen soul an equal position of spiritual authority over our mind, heart, and body is akin to insanity. However, the orchestrational power inherent to a spousal partnership, designed to mirror the first partnership, whispers seductively to every sovereign determined to orchestrate a unique world within God's world.

The only sensible reason for risking the dangers of marriage is to unite two unique world makers together in bringing forth the same unique world. Consequently, it is best for those who desire to take pleasure, procreation, and cohabitation from a partner to achieve those ends without yielding creative authority over their inner and material realms. In fact, this is exactly how fallen souls approach marriage. Takers enter into matrimony intent on keeping their partner from accessing their world while seditiously striving to gain access to their partner's world. Once either soul gets into their partner's world, they'll plunder remorselessly. Then, the retribution of their spouse will be swift and brutal. The warfare resulting between two takers bound within one unified inner realm is both terrifying to behold and captivating to watch.

If we seek to take pleasure, procreation, or cohabitation from another, then it is best to remain unmarried. However, if we seek to make a unique world, then it is best to intentionally design a marital partnership that mirrors the first partnership. Consequently, melding the spiritual, inner, and material realms of two spiritual beings into one flesh is an act that, once begun, should never be undone.

Melding two fleshly forms into one marital engine results in both souls having full ownership over the same spiritual, inner, and material realms. If either is an unrepentant world taker, then marriage should not even be considered. However, if both souls are repentant and growing world makers, then the inherent benefits of permanently uniting one masculine body to one feminine body will result in the orchestration of one unique world authoritatively shared by two unique world makers.

The souls dedicated, defiant, and determined enough to create their own unique world will risk the dangers of living out their own unique characterization of the first partnership. For such awakened creators, the Kingdom's soul checks offer vital protection. The first check essential for marriage is the creator's code. In fact, marriage necessitates the only acceptable alteration to the creator's code. As marriage is two souls orchestrating the same unique world, the code's use of the word "my" is simply replaced with the word "our." The resulting creator's code of marriage reads as follows; "Our world serves our intentions, our partners' intentions, and our Creator's intentions while obstructing anyone attempting to be the One."

Living by the creator's code of marriage requires each spouse to orchestrate one world, fulfilling the world-making intentions of two as if they were one. Additionally, the code further stipulates that the couple's resulting world must serve the intentions of all partners that both spouses bring to the union. The code further requires that both partners take one another's knowledge of God's intentions into consideration. Finally, the creator's code of marriage requires each to obstruct their soul, their partner's soul, and all souls from trying to be like God.

The second check vital for marriage is the perpetual acknowledgment of one another's soul identities. Amidst the intimate bond of marriage, each partner must retain their individual position as a distinct, separate, and inviolate spiritual authority. Anatomical equality does not exist in the material realm, where every snowflake, leaf, and human being is different. However, spiritual equality does exist since each soul holds the exact same spiritual position beneath God's authority.

An individual's soul identity reveals how they uniquely experience, embody, and express their Creator. Marriage honors the unique spiritual nature of both as each perpetually acknowledges one another's soul identity. Since each soul is originally born as the only authority within their world, it is easy to forget that our spouse is an equal and unassailable spiritual authority within one shared world. Continually acknowledging one another's unique spiritual nature garners vital personal dignity amidst a union so intimate that it will ceaselessly threaten to dissolve each partner's sovereignty, individuality, and liberty.

The Kingdom's final soul check for marriage is the three orders. The Subduing, Filling, and Ruling Orders help each spouse to discover, appreciate, and respect their partner. Knowing our spouse's mental, emotional, or physical expertise is vital for admiring them not only as a spiritual authority but as a creative authority as well.

Perceiving human beings as warriors, wizards, and wills is what helps the unmarried find an ideal spouse, and the married realize why they were attracted to one another in the first place. Every creator is naturally drawn toward a partner who wields a creative expertise that complements their creative insufficiency. Without profound thoughts, potent emotions, and powerful actions, a unique world will fail. Therefore, every human being intuitively selects a spouse from the order focused on the inner realm of thought, emotion, or action where they personally struggle. As an example, the world maker who is a wizard with a secondary talent as a ruler and who struggles as a warrior will naturally desire a spouse who is a warrior with a secondary talent as a ruler and who struggles as a wizard. The ideal marital union is where each spouse's creative expertise covers their partner's creative weakness while both share the same secondary talent. As a result, each will then have a personal position of creative expertise within the marriage that serves their spouse's creative insufficiency. Additionally, both will also share the third inner creative domain as creative equals. When a couple acknowledges the Kingdom's three orders, they'll find the means to clarify where each spouse is a creative expert, where each spouse needs their partner's creative expertise, and where both may work together as creative equals.

Marriage arrives when two souls give their two minds, two hearts, and two bodies to one another for the explicit purpose of creating one unique world that will fulfill the principal purpose of both amidst an orchestrational scope that neither could've even dreamt of achieving individually. Such an impossibility is only possible because God made one body to portray the Masculine Creator and a second to portray the feminine creation so each human being—through marriage—might fully engage in world-making. Ambitious souls risk the dangers of marriage because they desire the best means available for orchestrating their unique world, and marriage holds, by far, the greatest potential for generating profound thoughts, potent emotions, and powerful actions.

The story depicting the first partnership provides us with only bits and pieces of information regarding how the Masculine One and the feminine one originally united to bring forth the first unique world. Ultimately, each couple will design their own unique characterization of the first partnership. The only non-negotiable is that there must only be one masculine creator and one feminine creation consensually uniting together to orchestrate the same unique world.

Fortunately, studying the short narrative articulating the first partnership does reveal the fundamental functionality of how the masculine and the feminine work together. The first partnership exerted two beneficially opposed forces: push and pull. God pushed while creation pulled. During each day of the first seven days, God pushed creation apart to make visionary, meaningful, and purposeful separations amidst her atoms. Simultaneously, creation responded with an unending pull to keep all her separated atoms united as a cohesive whole, which permanently affixed her Creator's separations. A human couple does likewise by having their male body push God's world apart so their female body might pull the remaining atoms back together into an approximation of the world they both desire.

The male body exists to push like the Creator, for predetermined outcomes. In marriage, a man's body is no longer his own but his wife's as well. Consequently, the male body is the material vehicle desired by both souls to push their combined world-making intentions out into God's world. A woman chooses a man with a body capable of mentally, emotionally, and physically pushing her world-making intentions into Mother Nature. Therefore, a woman offers her body to a man so she might gain intimate access to his body so that she might inspire him to push aggressively for the visionary, meaningful, and purposeful separations needed to distinguish her world from God's world.

A female, as the embodiment of Mother Nature, exists to pull together a unique world from amidst God's world. A woman's body is designed to irresistibly attract every nearby atom and pull each into a never-before-seen pattern of orbital beauty. Consequently, a man chooses his wife based on her ability to attract. Once married, a woman's body is no longer hers alone. A husband is eager to integrate his orchestrational intentions into his wife's attractive form. Without a woman's alluring body, a male is largely incapable of holding together a unique world. The reason bachelor pads are always so sparsely appointed is that a man's ability to repulse material objects is several magnitudes higher than his ability to attract material objects. When a soul only has access to a masculine body, everything he pursues unerringly moves away from him, making it extremely taxing to hold onto anything. Consequently, the only force strong enough to counteract a man's repulsive nature is the irresistible allure of a feminine partner.

God gave us two material forms so that each soul might have the means to push their way into His world and then pull together their own unique human world. Marriage gives each soul the opportunity to direct the two forms designed by God to power world-making. The only catch is that acquiring the body we're not born with requires relinquishing exclusive ownership over the body that we are born with. When two married souls direct their two beneficially opposed bodies toward the same shared end, they'll work together to push and pull upon God's world until they succeed in bringing forth their world.

As the embodiment of creation, a woman's pull is all-inclusive. Like gravity, she's always pulling on everything, and she cannot turn it off. However, her masculine partner will aggressively repulse the majority of atoms that a woman is trying to pull closer. As finite beings destined to orchestrate a finite world, a couple must remain selective regarding which anatomical objects they include. A male body is ideally suited to define, decide, and dictate which atoms to repulse. Still, a man must not treat the repulsed atoms as evil but merely as unnecessary for the couple's intended world. At the same time, his wife will allure, arouse, and augment every remaining atom into its own distinctive orbital pattern to steadily bring about the orchestration of the couple's intended world.

Amidst our fallen age, a husband serves his wife by pushing away most material objects to obstruct her from trying to replace creation. A woman pulls on everything, as in the entire universe, often with little understanding of how deeply this offends Mother Nature. Fallen women routinely compete with one another over who is the supreme puller. However, a man will innately strive to restrain his wife from competing against creation for the central position of anatomical allure over the entire material universe. While competition between women is vicious, a man is right to fear his wife getting into a spat with mother.

Despite a man's repulsive service, it will pain his wife to have so many good anatomical treasures pushed away. Like creation, a woman desires to include everything within her world. A fallen wife will end up resenting a pushy partner who is obstructing her from placing the entire material universe beneath her orbital sway. Only while living by the creator's code will a woman recognize her husband's repulsive efforts as a service, not only to his world-making intentions but hers as well.

As the embodiment of the Creator, a man's push is selective. God made the male body capable of exerting extreme bursts of repulsive strength. However, a man must target, activate, and execute each push with deliberate focus. Consequently, a woman's unending pull acts as a safeguard against her husband's outward expansion. She doesn't want her man striving to conquer the entire universe, so he might present himself as God. Therefore, the inevitable moment a man must relent from his outward aggression, his wife's ceaseless allure will steadily draw him back toward the epicenter of their world, which would be her. Only when living by the creator's code, will a husband recognize his wife's irresistible allure as not merely pulling him back to her world but his as well.

The deeper danger inherent to marriage grows vividly apparent once a couple starts pushing and pulling directly upon one another. Whenever two beneficially opposed forces touch, sparks fly. Although sparks signify the presence of power, they also reveal the ineffective use of that power. Relational sparks merely signify that a negative pushing force and a positive pulling force are interacting. Sadly, the spousal sparks that naturally accompany newly formed couples often fade rapidly, revealing how ineffective humanity remains at uniting our two polarized natures in a way that generates flowing currents of orchestrational power.

Spousal sparks, and the potential for world-making power they infer, do not exist for our personal amusement. Marital power generation exists to enable a couple's world-making effort. Using the passion, pleasure, and power of a spousal union to satiate the infinite spiritual emptiness within one's soul will always destroy a marital union. God gave us the ability to inwardly unite with a spouse to empower our material world-making efforts, not to replace our spiritual union with Him.

A couple's job is to direct the sparks that naturally fly between their two bodies toward world-making. The first partnership reveals the unfathomable power generation that arises between a masculine pusher and feminine puller. The provocative power of marriage, although scaled down significantly, carries the same potential for generating the orchestrational currents needed to animate, and then illuminate, a unique world. However, if a couple does not channel the initial sparks of their union toward world-making, then the power generation between their two bodies will falter and eventually fade. Without a world-making effort to power, a couple's marital engine will steadily grind to a halt, resulting in a union that can no longer even generate sparks.

Marriage exists to power the orchestration of one unique world for two unique world makers. Whenever two souls with two beneficially opposed bodies commit to creating the same unique world, their spousal sparks will naturally swell into the conductive currents that will flow out from in between their two souls, through their united inner realm, and into their personal portion of creation's material realm. However, before a couple can direct their opposing forces materially, they must learn to do so inwardly. Even more importantly, before a couple can inwardly direct their push and pull, they must first embody those two forces spiritually.

Existing as two spiritual beings of polarizing power requires each soul to ceaselessly increase their polarized union with God. Our species feels perpetually powerless because we refuse to consensually reconnect with Power. While living in a spiritual union with God, each soul will know the boundless masculine push of Infinite Fullness. Simultaneously, each soul will also discover their boundless feminine pull as a void of infinite emptiness. Consequently, each spouse must learn to pull upon Infinite Fullness, as His infinite emptiness, to allure their Creator deeper into the epicenter of their soul. Then, as a feminine creation of the Masculine Creator, each sovereign soul may express their own spiritual partnership with the Spouse, with a spouse.

Since each soul lives with the Masculine Creator as His feminine creation, each spouse experiences, and may then begin to exert, both negative masculine push and positive feminine pull. Once married, both partners gain the advantage of being able to focus on the force that their body is naturally attuned to project. A spiritual soul does not have a sex. Only material bodies come predetermined with an orientation toward conducting negative masculine repulsion or positive feminine attraction. Each sexless soul may diverge from their body's natural attunement to masculine push or feminine pull, but they only do so to the detriment of their body's world-making potential.

A woman's body is capable of pushing aggressively but not to the peak levels of exertion possible through a male body. Likewise, a man's body is capable of pulling alluringly, but definitely not with the scale and unending force of a woman's body. Orchestrating a unique world is best achieved when one is forcefully pushing God's world apart, and the other is forcefully pulling what remains back together. Pushing into God's world is hard work, as is pulling each lingering element back together into a customized landscape of anatomical approximation.

The forceful nature of push and pull must flow from God's spiritual realm, through a couple's united inner realm, and then out into creation's material realm. Each spouse's soul must authoritatively direct both dangerous forces outward. Fortunately, our two human forms desire to serve in this effort because God designed them to facilitate a spousal partnership of world-making power based upon the first partnership of world-making power. The only thing a male and a female body require are two spiritual sovereigns capable of forcefully directing them toward making the same unique world. Once each partner's soul is emanating one of the two original forces in alignment with their body's natural attunement, the couple's orchestrational power will steadily build between them in anticipation of powering their unique world.

Every couple has experienced the power that sparks to life between a male and a female body. As fallen beings, we greedily consume our spousal sparks in a futile attempt to animate and illuminate our lifeless souls. Unfortunately, redirecting the conductive currents of marriage into two infinitely empty spiritual voids is utterly catastrophic for both bodies, the marriage, and a couple's fledgling world.

Instead of draining one's marriage of orchestrational power, resurrected souls turn their infinite spiritual emptiness upon Infinite Fullness. As a result, each resurrected soul will come to their marriage bursting with more passion, pleasure, and power than their spousal union could ever handle. Therefore, the foundation for each marital union is the spiritual union each soul experiences with God. Marriage simply provides a couple with the means to materially express the power-inducing intimacy that each is spiritually enjoying with the Soulmate.

As long as a couple does not revert to taking, the power generation between their two bodies will rise indefinitely. World makers will elegantly direct their spousal sparks to swell into the conductive currents they need to animate and illuminate their own unique world. A couple succeeds in turning their spousal sparks into orchestrational power once their two minds, hearts, and bodies are producing thoughts, emotions, and actions that are several orders of magnitude beyond anything they could've achieved individually. As a result, every couple will realize they've already tasted the ascendant wonders of the marital engine.

Often, an aging couple will reminisce fondly regarding their early days. The bliss, butterflies, and beauty of young love are poetic frames for orchestrational power. If we're honest, we'll have to admit that the nostalgia we sense toward young love is really about the mental, emotional, and physical orchestrational power we briefly tasted and let slip away, resulting in a drastic decrease in our world-making potential.

When a couple is in love, their two minds, hearts, and bodies first spark and then transform into an engine of frightening orchestrational power. As a result, young love is often judged as a form of temporary insanity. When two polarized minds, hearts, and bodies start melding together into one supercharged orchestrational engine without two spiritual authorities capable of effectively directing that power, things get out of hand pretty quickly. Because of this, the excitement experienced by young lovers often fades rapidly. Once Mother Nature notices two souls emanating dangerous levels of orchestrational power beyond their ability to direct effectively and efficiently, she is forced to step in and unplug the couple's marital engine. The remorse we then feel after falling out of love is rooted in having briefly known, and then lost, the means to produce the profound thoughts, potent emotions, and powerful actions needed for making our unique world.

Although marriage is important, unmarried individuals may still orchestrate their own unique world. However, unmarried individuals still model the first partnership. An unmarried individual uses their spiritual soul to push and their inner realm to pull toward producing their own unique world within God's world. Although unmarried is where we all begin, each world maker senses the limitless potential of a more robust portrayal of the first partnership. Despite marriage posing the greatest danger to the orchestration of our own unique world, it also holds the greatest potential for orchestrating our own unique world.

God entrusted humanity with two bodies for a reason. He wants each couple to live out their own unique characterization of the first partnership so that they might power the orchestration of their own unique world within His world. As a result, the couple who lives by the code, upholds one another as spiritual authorities, and lives as complimentary creative experts will wield a marital engine of limitless orchestrational power designed by God to animate and illuminate a uniquely human world within His world of unique worlds.

Section 9
The Abilities of Being

Melding together the creator's perspective, doctrines, and Kingdom will now highlight for us the three spiritual abilities vital for orchestrating a unique world within God's world. First, each world maker exudes their own aura of inevitability regarding the orchestration of their sovereign domain. Second, each world maker also emanates God's impossibility requiring them to intimately and daily commune with Mother Nature to support her orchestrational efforts. Most importantly, each world maker embodies holistic responsibility for themselves, the church, and our entire species so that they might lead all toward being a race of unique world makers who, together, are bringing forth the world of unique worlds desired by our World Maker.

Chapter 25
Heartfelt Inevitability

Once we consent to be spiritually touched, shaped, and breathed into by God to conceive a unique spiritual being from within our soul, we'll immediately find the directional flow of our life inverting. As fallen beings, we strive to take from creation what we hope will animate and illuminate our souls. However, after surrendering unconditionally to God—so He might bring forth one bearing a never-before-seen likeness of His spiritual uniqueness—we no longer need anything from material creation. Instead, as a resurrected spiritual being, we emanate the inevitably that, as a unique world maker, we exist to animate and illuminate our own unique world. Therefore, the moment-by-moment spiritual insemination of our soul through a timeless, spaceless, and matterless union of faith with our Creator is the quintessential, present-moment experience that perpetually transforms us from being a replicated world taker into a unique world maker.

The moment we awaken as a living, world-making creator an aura of inevitability begins to emanate from within us. After all, a world maker exists to make their own unique world. As a result, once our soul is communing with the World Maker, we'll inevitably do what He has already done. Additionally, Mother Nature is designed by God to attune to, partner with, and orchestrate a unique world around every one of His unique ones. Therefore, the moment we awaken as a spiritual world maker, our material mother will intuitively reach toward us so that we might begin authoritatively ruling, filling, and subduing our personal portion of her into our own unique world so that she might further fulfill her desire to grow toward becoming God's world of unique worlds.

Inexperienced creators misstep when they try to force creation to bring forth their desired world. Instead, a more effective method is to let Mother Nature pursue us rather than frantically trying to pursue her. God has already impelled creation to serve the knowledge, desires, and intentions of each sovereign soul through the Great Imperative. Presently, all our mother requires are those who are worthy and capable of authoritatively leading her toward fulfilling her knowledge, her desire, and her intent to become God's world of unique worlds. Therefore, each world maker emanating the inevitability that, as a unique world maker they exist to make their own unique world, will not need to force creation to do what she already wants to do.

The urgency that each fallen soul senses toward having their own unique world is the same urgency our ancestors sensed toward clothing their naked bodies. Without a unique world covering our lightless, loveless, and lifeless soul, we each feel exposed as one who has failed to be like the World Maker. Consequently, each tainted soul is desperate for a material covering that will make them look like God. However, after a soul is spiritually inseminated by the World Maker—to conceive from within them a unique world maker—there is no longer a need for a material covering. Instead, an inseminated soul simply radiates their own inevitability that, as a unique world maker, they exist to inseminate creation with what she needs to conceive their unique world so that she might further grow toward becoming God's world of unique worlds.

As a resurrected spiritual being, we don't do anything. Instead, as resurrected spiritual beings, we exist to uniquely be something, somewhere, and someone. As a result, there is no need to impress upon creation the urgency of orchestrating our unique world, particularly since she already wants to orchestrate our unique world. Pressuring our material mother to do what she already wants to do will only further confirm for her that we remain a replicated world taker and not a unique world maker. Our soul's job is to receive our own unique likeness of the World Maker so that we might radiate our new nature into material creation. Then, Mother Nature will see to her work of enveloping us with a unique world suitable to our growing likeness of Uniqueness.

As timeless, spaceless, and matterless spiritual beings we have no need to hurry. This is good because it will take time to heal the partnership between our fallen soul and Mother Nature. As only recently inseminated ones, we must endeavor to woo our material mother with our newfound spiritual likeness by simply being inevitable rather than trying to pressure her toward the instantaneous manifestation of a perfect world.

As recovering world takers, the ideal approach is not to focus on the future world we desire but instead to focus on the present world we already have. Creation expects us to genuinely appreciate the world of darkness, decay, and death she's already surrounded us with as a good and pleasing approximation of our previously lightless, loveless, and lifeless soul. If we do not fully acknowledge the goodness of all our mother's past work, then we should not expect her to exert herself in any future effort.

Creation expects each human creator to treat her how the Creator did during the first seven days. Mother Nature was good, is good, and will always remain good. Everything creation was before our fall was good. Everything she has become because of our fall is still good. And even the death she will ultimately experience because of us is also good. Only after a soul begins to affectionately embrace all of Mother Nature's present material approximations of their soul's original state as a lifeless world taker will she also consider beginning to materially approximate their soul's present state as a growing world maker.

As fallen ones, we often assume that creation has rejected us as her authoritatively endowed rulers, fillers, and subduers. In fact, creation has never stopped orchestrating a world around us that will accurately express us. The only party guilty of rejection is us. We've perpetually denied creation's request to fully approximate our lifeless spiritual nature. Understandably, no untouched soul wants a world displaying them as a lightless, loveless, and lifeless void of infinite spiritual emptiness. As a result, fallen souls demand the instantaneous manifestation of a perfect world so that they might display themselves as the Perfect One. Unfortunately, creation can only birth a material world that expresses the spiritual being we already are, not the One we one day hope to be.

Fallen humanity has unknowingly put creation in an impossible situation. God designed her and charged her to accurately express every spiritual being with their own material world. However, as her authoritatively endowed rulers, fillers, and subduers, we've categorically denied creation permission to accurately express our lifeless spiritual nature. As a result, creation is stuck trying to simultaneously fulfill the incompatible desires of her Creator and her fallen human creators. Such authoritative incongruence upon our feminine mother has compelled her to try to do both as she gives rise to a material world around each tainted soul that briefly enables them to look, feel, and act like God, only to have it all abruptly collapsing back into her void-like dust.

It is inevitable that a creator will create. As creators, we remain the inspirational source of the world around us, both as lifeless souls of darkness, decay, and death and as resurrected beings of illumination, animation, and regeneration. The world surrounding each soul always corresponds to their spiritual likeness. Attempting to deceive, manipulate, and force creation's approximations away from evil and toward good will only serve to further reveal our nature as a taker, thereby obligating our mother to hasten the implosion of our world.

Once our soul is touched by the Creator to conceive from within us our own likeness of His world-making uniqueness, there is no need to change anything about our partnership with creation. Mother Nature materially approximated us as fallen ones, and she will do likewise once we're unique ones. However, creation does not wish her past material efforts to be discarded. As a result, we must recognize all Mother Nature's approximations as good by allowing every single aspect of her to persist as she sees fit. Therefore, the unique world orchestrated around our soul amidst our presently cursed, corrupted, and condemned age will not be a perfect world but one that will sublimely fuse together our fallen past, our present struggle, and our future hope.

Each resurrected world maker must maintain an unwavering acknowledgment that each one of creation's material approximations are good, as she synchronously and simultaneously expresses their original state of spiritual death alongside their present state of spiritual life. However, a resurrected sovereign may assist Mother Nature in the latter by giving her unilateral permission to express their soul as she sees fit, an allowance we'll each find ourselves utterly terrified to give. Only after giving creation unrestricted permission to express our spiritual likeness as she desires will we discover the depths to which we've been hindering her from becoming God's world of unique worlds.

Emanating inevitability as a world maker redefines our past, reestablishes our present, and repurposes our future. We cannot afford to forget our fallen past as world takers, our present charge as world makers, and our future hope of partnering with the Creator in orchestrating one of the unique worlds required for His eternal world of unique worlds. Therefore, existing as a creator of orchestrational inevitability is the first spiritual ability wielded by one destined to make their own world within God's world.

Chapter 26
Daily Impossibility

It was impossible for material creation to express the spiritual Creator. However, the sheer impossibility of the task aroused Mother Nature to exert herself in a universal effort. As resurrected spiritual beings, we also uniquely embody God's impossibility. Therefore, we also follow God's original model of intimate orchestration by daily speaking, touching, and breathing our impossible likeness into creation. Learning such artistry does not arrive by reading an ancient story but by allowing God to timelessly speak, touch, and breathe His impossible likeness into our souls. Then, we may do to creation what the Creator is doing to us.

Arousing creation to express our impossible spiritual nature with a unique material world requires following God's original method of a segmented orchestrational effort. The seven uniques is a blueprint that helps us map out our own life-long plan for orchestrational success. However, creation requires more than a plan. She requires intimate and daily communion with a creator who has a plan.

As the original feminine partner, Mother Nature demands that we demonstrate our commitment to her with deliberate attentiveness. More specifically, our material mother expects us to put her survival and comfort before our orchestration intentions. Therefore, as Mother Nature's masculine spiritual partners, we woo creation to our world-making effort by first serving her anatomical needs. Only daily, intimate communion between each spiritual creator and material creation will result in the orchestration of every unique world that Mother Nature needs to become God's world of unique worlds.

A general method for steadily wooing creation as a world-making partner is the sixty-thirty-ten principle. Each day sixty percent of our time should go toward survival, thirty percent toward comfort, and only ten percent toward orchestrating our unique world. A big turn-off for Mother Nature is the soul who is so desperate to orchestrate their own world that they imperil her survival and comfort as God's world.

Spending sixty percent of each day on survival appears daunting until we realize that sleep is the major chunk of this investment. While sleeping, our anatomical mind, heart, and body are temporarily removed from our direct oversight so that they might regenerate their creative capabilities without our meddlesome spiritual interference. World making requires profound thoughts, potent emotions, and powerful actions. Without fully relinquishing our inner realm to creation's care for seven to ten hours each day, we cannot expect our mind, heart, and body to orchestrate anything that will express our unique world-making likeness.

Following a good night's sleep, the remaining four to seven hours each day that we set aside for our survival should go toward personal hygiene, proper diet, reasonable exercise, and whatever else we find indispensable to our survival. Creation is always attentively watching how we treat our mind, heart, and body. Our mother has entrusted the most treasured aspects of herself to our care because she wants to be touched by those who are being touched by Life. Creation knows firsthand the abundance that flows from the World Maker's touch. She expects something similar from each world maker who is being touched by the World Maker.

After spending sixty percent of our day focused on survival, we may then turn the next thirty percent of our day toward comfort. Attending to our comfort-generating relationships, possessions, and environments takes time. However, our mind, heart, and body need a comfortable existence if we expect them to bring forth the profound thoughts, potent emotions, and powerful actions needed for making our unique world.

As timeless, spaceless, and matterless spiritual beings, we do not directly experience the strenuous demands of orchestration. Only our mind, heart, and body endure the strain of approximating our impossible spiritual nature. Solidifying the distinction between our soul and our inner realm of thought, emotion, and action is essential for those who wish to treat each of the anatomical components of Mother Nature entrusted to their care with the proper respect, appreciation, and love.

Creation does all the material expressing on our behalf. Our job is to spiritually be someone worth materially expressing. Only after Mother Nature begins to mentally see, emotionally feel, and physically experience how we're cultivating comfortable survival within our inner realm will she consider enveloping us with a larger portion of her material realm so we might lead her toward making our unique world to take her one step closer toward becoming God's world of unique worlds.

Creation wants to surround each spiritual being with a world that materially glorifies what, where, and who they are. However, our mother needs to get to know us before she can express us. While we daily work on creation's survival and comfort, we're giving our foremost material partner a low-pressure environment to interact with our inevitable and impossible spiritual being. Just as how we do not begin a spousal courtship by presenting a formal proposal of legally binding marriage, we likewise begin our courtship with creation by putting aside our grand orchestrational intentions so we might work intently, intimately, and daily upon her survival and comfort.

A creator does not demand. A creator serves. While we serve in the survival and comfort of creation, we're giving each of mother's atoms the opportunity they need to get to know us so they might begin reorienting their orbital patterns around our unique nature. Attending to creation's comfortable survival is what allows us to gently speak, authoritatively touch, and affectionally breathe our impossible spiritual nature into our orchestrational mother.

Creation is not interested in our plan; she's interested in our person. Plans don't make worlds. Persons make worlds. Our foremost material partner wants each spiritual world maker—who has a plan—to lead her toward making one of the unique worlds that she needs to become her Beloved's world of unique worlds.

Limiting our orchestrational efforts to one to three hours each day is a realistic mark for growing world makers. Doing so will keep us from overburdening our inner realm and creation's material realm. Such a stark restraint upon our orchestrational efforts will also reveal how desperate we remain for a material covering for our vacuous soul. Each one who needs a world is still a taker and remains in desperate need of the World Maker. After all, the Creator did not need a world—He wanted a world, which compelled Him to give creation permission to materially approximate His inevitable and impossible spiritual being.

During the twenty-one to twenty-three hours each day we're focused on creation's survival and comfort, we'll inevitably expose our shameful desperation for the instantaneous manifestation of a perfect world. Each taker is frantic to hide their failure to be like God behind a world that portrays them as God. Therefore, abstaining from twenty-four-hour a day campaign toward orchestrational success is vital for exposing how much we still retain the nature of the world taker and further require the insemination of the World Maker.

In the beginning, God treated creation with gentleness, appreciation, and love while simultaneously existing as the spiritual Being of Impossible Inevitability. Then, He entrusted creation to our care under the condition that we remain at His side so that we might learn how to touch our mother with our own form of gentleness, appreciation, and love, as He touches our soul as Gentleness, Appreciation, and Love.

Partnering with creation does not require us to be sappy, soft, and safe creators. As resurrected beings, we bear a unique characterization of God's likeness, causing us to emanate our own unassailable spiritual authority as we treat creation with gentleness, appreciation, and love. Such a paradox arouses creation's desire to partner with us, reminiscent of how she originally partnered with God. Women, as those who embody Mother Nature, desire a masculine partner who is both gentle, appreciative, and loving as well as authoritative, unassailable, and dangerous. Fallen men naturally see such a paradox as incongruent, but only because they've failed to spiritually live with—and receive their own likeness of—the Paradox. Therefore, as creators, we affectionately tend to creation's survival and comfort while simultaneously existing as a being of dangerous orchestrational authority to arouse Mother Nature to partner with us in a manner like she first partnered with God.

A creator serves creation's survival and comfort so that she might do likewise in serving their orchestrational intentions, a skill we first learn by allowing the Creator to do to us what we desire to do to creation. As we attend to Mother Nature's survival and comfort, we're simultaneously radiating our orchestrational intentions. The more inevitable and impossible we are, the more arousing we become. At the same time, the more inevitable and impossible we are, the more kindly and attentively we must treat creation. A world maker never demands material results. Instead, a world maker simply exists as a being that creation will demand to express with material results.

As every soul eventually discovers, surviving comfortably without a visionary and meaningful purpose is depressing. Therefore, as creators, we direct ninety percent of each day toward ensuring creation's survival and comfort to prime the atoms around our soul for a grand orchestrational effort in the final ten percent. During the one to three hours each day set aside for orchestration, we commit all toward our present progress within our seven uniques. Aiming ultimately at the orchestration of our unique world is what gives our comfortable survival its visionary, meaningful purpose.

Following the sixty-thirty-ten principle toward fulfilling our seven uniques will steadily enrich and expand the way we experience survival, comfort, and orchestration. For example, while pursuing our first unique, we'll design the mental, emotional, and physical habits essential for our unique body. However, after achieving our first unique, everything we've successfully orchestrated will end up integrated into either the sixty percent of our day focused on survival or the thirty percent focused on comfort. Then, the remaining ten percent of our day will be freed up to work on our second unique. This process will repeat throughout all seven uniques until each orchestrated element is integrated completely into the singular whole of comfortable survival that is our world. After completing our seventh unique, our body will return to dust, prohibiting any further orchestration. However, if we've elegantly integrated all seven uniques of our world into one cohesive whole of comfortable survival, then our legacy will endure far beyond our orchestrational lifetime.

As beings of inevitable impossibility, we lead creation toward a comfortable survival to prepare her for and lead her into our grand orchestrational effort. We do not need creation. Everything we need, as a soul of infinite emptiness, is spiritually provided by Infinite Fullness. As a result, a growing world maker will slowly discover that it is Mother Nature who needs them, as a spiritual being of impossible inevitability, to lead her toward bringing forth one of the unique worlds that she needs to fulfill her desire to become God's world of unique worlds.

Chapter 27
Holistic Responsibility

Responsibility is the ability to respond. When we take responsibility, we take control of our ability to respond to the happenings within our spiritual, inner, and material realms. Accepting responsibility has nothing to do with accepting fault. The comprehensive mess brought about by humanity's fall is not holistically our individual fault. However, as individuals, we each have the ability to respond holistically to the comprehensive mess brought about by our species. As creators, we do not control the happenings of our triune existence. Still, we can control how we respond. Consequently, how we respond to our spiritual, inner, and material surroundings demonstrates our likeness, or our lack of likeness, to the World Maker.

The inclusive scope of one's response reveals a creator's level of maturity. As newly resurrected spiritual beings, we initially learn how to respond in ways that only uphold our orchestrational intentions. Doing so is important. As sovereign, individual, and liberty-loving world makers, we must begin each interaction with another world maker by unabashedly presenting our intent to orchestrate our own unique world alongside their unique world so that, together, we might orchestrate two unique worlds for God's world of unique worlds. If we do not, then our potential world-making partners will assume that our intent is to take their world and make it our world so we might rule, fill, and subdue all worlds. World-making partnerships cannot form unless the intentions of all involved world makers are laid bare for collective consideration.

It's important to note that no one ever selflessly serves anyone else's world-making intentions. Even God serves humanity so that we will, in turn, serve Him. It just so happens that serving God's intentions also results in us getting everything we intend. God's ability to respond in a way that fulfills His intentions while synchronously, simultaneously, and equally fulfilling the intentions of each of His partners is the inspiring benchmark for each soul who embraces holistic responsibility.

Every response God has, is, and ever will form always serves the deepest orchestrational intentions of everything and everyone. The reason we so often disagree with God's responses is that we cannot see how each of His responses are leading us toward what we want. Of course, the deeper issue is that we don't even know what we actually want, which inhibits us from recognizing the opportunity God is offering us with each response He forms.

We begin growing our responsibility by authoritatively upholding only our personal orchestrational intentions. However, it is vital that we continue growing into a more holistically responsible creator. After all, every world maker bringing forth their own unique world expects our responses to at least consider, if not work toward fulfilling, their world-making intentions.

The undulating anatomical expanse of Mother Nature enveloping every soul ripples with the impact of everyone's spiritual, inner, and material responses. Since creation's anatomical splendor links together every soul, a response from anyone affects everyone. Consequently, a mature spiritual being is one who intentionally forms their responses in a way that will fulfill their orchestrational intentions, creation's orchestrational intentions, all humanity's orchestrational intentions, and even the Creator's orchestrational intentions. At first, such a standard may seem impossible to attain. Still, a being of inevitable impossible responsibility will rise to the challenge. Additionally, walking alongside the One who is Inevitable Impossible Responsibility will also help.

Every creator seeks a leader capable of bringing them into a grand world-making effort which will result in them discovering, forming, and executing their own grand world-making effort. Ultimately, God is the Leader. However, those who live with the Leader will live as a leader. Therefore, the being who responds to life in a way that fulfills the orchestrational intentions of all will inspirationally lead all toward being a race of unique worlds makers bringing forth a world of unique worlds.

Once we're growing our ability to respond more holistically to the intentions of all, then we're ready to take a seat at the Director's table of God's family business. Partnering with our Creator requires further development of our ability to respond from a position of timeless, spaceless, and matterless eternity. Although sitting at the Director's table might appear as the pinnacle of holistic responsibility, it is, in fact, only the beginning. Once we start responding as a being who exists first and foremost in the spiritual realm, we dramatically increase the impact that our responses exert upon time, space, and matter.

Responding to life in a way that upholds only our personal orchestrational intentions is worthy of respect. However, responding to life in a way that upholds God's intentions, creation's intentions, and every human being's intentions—alongside our own intentions—is worthy of reverence. As a world maker grows, so does their ability to respond more holistically. Responding in a way that considers humanity's lost past, present struggle, and future hope is the beginning of a sovereign who is a growing orchestrational authority of holistic responsibility. Contextualizing our holistic responses amidst the moment-by-moment complexities inherent to the spiritual, inner, and material realms is an ability that every world maker will be growing across the boundless expanse of eternity.

While seated at the Director's table, a spiritual creator exercises their ability to respond in a way that benefits all. Orchestrating a world of unique worlds requires human creators, creation, and the Creator to work together. A mature sovereign responds to life in a way that leads everyone toward a realistic partnership based upon the past, to aid the present, and in service of our shared future. Making oneself the binding epicenter of a grand orchestrational partnership is God's strategy. Those who live with Him will do likewise.

No one needs to sacrifice their orchestrational intentions for the greater good. No world maker must ever sacrifice their world. God's world of unique worlds—that Mother Nature desires to become—demands that each one form, oversee, and protect their own world from within God's world. As sovereign souls mature, each must learn to stand up for both their orchestrational intentions and the orchestrational intentions of all, synchronously, simultaneously, and equally. After all, the supreme goal is not only our world, but our world independently interconnected in interdependence with every world amidst God's world. Although this may appear to echo the fallen view of sacrificing for the greater good it is not. The best way to ensure the significance, reverence, and permanence of our world is to ensure it is invaluable to every other world maker's world within God's world of unique worlds.

An example of holistic responsibility is the Kingdom of Creators. The Kingdom of Creators is a holistic response to the disaster of humanity, the complexity of creation, and the unchanging principal purpose of the Creator. First, the Kingdom acknowledges that each human being is born as a replicated world taker who still desires to become a unique world maker. Consequently, the creator's code, soul identities, and the three orders are all responses intentionally designed to check everyone's nature as a taker and lead all toward the World Maker.

The Kingdom of Creators is also a response to the complexity of creation. As fallen beings, we do not treat our material mother as a partner. She is a thing that we use and discard at our discretion rather than the only material partner available for our orchestrational efforts. Therefore, the Kingdom of Creators responds to this with the seven uniques, the seven battalions, and the first partnership. The seven uniques exist to guide each soul toward orchestrating their world in a manner that respects creation's material realm of time, space, and matter. Then, the seven battalions exist to inspire all committed creators to join together on a grand scale to work toward the survival, comfort, and orchestration of every soul still held within our mother's affectionate material embrace. And finally, the Kingdom's focus on the first partnership exists to provoke all committed creators to risk restructuring their most vital human partnership toward glorifying creation's original and powerful union with her Creator.

The Kingdom of Creators is also a response to the unchanging principal purpose of God. Often in the past, the church has fallen into complacency amidst the convenience of writing off the present age as evil, so we might sit back in anticipation of the good age yet to come. However, God's principal purpose remains unwavering. He wants to grow world makers in the present fallen age as well as in the coming resurrected age. The Kingdom responds to this by highlighting the paramount importance of each soul living presently as a responsible being of inevitable, world-making impossibility. Each resurrected spiritual creator must actively exercise their own authoritative nature in the service of God's unwavering principal purpose, so all might return to subduing, filling, and ruling their own personal portion of material creation to bring forth the world only they can make for God world of unique worlds.

How we respond is always telling, but more commonly, how we do not respond is even more telling. Letting creation respond, letting other human beings respond, and even letting our mind, heart, and body respond to the mess that we've spiritually wrought is the essence of an irresponsible being. Worse yet, sitting back and waiting for God to respond is utterly pathetic. Our Maker has already endowed each soul with the authority to respond to each spiritual, inner, and material possibility. Choosing not to respond with the authority of the Great Imperative, with the creative capabilities outlined in the Greatest Commandment, and the process of partnering laid out in the Great Commission negates us as world makers while disrespecting God's principal purpose.

Humanity's hesitancy toward authoritatively exercising holistic responsibility is not human. God's enemy has carefully cultivated our species toward being docile vessels. Due to his own spiritual, inner, and material impotence, the taker cannot allow humanity to rediscover who still holds the ruling, filling, and subduing authority over creation. The taker's authority is not his own; he took it—not from God, but from us. Those who dare to recall the Great Imperative will rediscover the unaltered heritage of subduing fire, filling water, and ruling light which remains exclusively endowed upon the human race.

Humanity's tendency toward irresponsibility is being sustained by a habitual pattern of blaming creation's material atoms for our spiritual corruption. Material sin is not the problem. Spiritual sinners are the problem. The self-aware soul recognizes that they, as an untouched void of infinite spiritual emptiness, are impelling creation to materially express all the darkness, decay, and death currently spreading across the globe. How we respond to such a damning revelation of reality will then determine everything we spiritually, inwardly, and materially create.

Acknowledging our untouched soul as a lifeless, spiritual void requires that we respond in a way that leads toward our personal spiritual fulfillment. Unfortunately, any solution that arises from within our void—to fill our void—will only result in an ever-increasing void. As a lightless, loveless, and lifeless soul, we each require the insemination of Infinite Fullness. Our Maker is the only one who may touch our vacuous void from within to prohibit any outside-in meddling so that we might then arise into our own untainted and never-before-seen likeness of the

World Maker. Consequently, unconditionally surrendering our souls to the Unknowable One is the response championed by the Kingdom of Creators. However, any who believes they've found their own alternative source of infinite spiritual fulfillment are free to respond accordingly.

The one who exercises holistic responsibility for their soul in the spiritual realm by opening themselves exclusively to the Soulmate is ready for greater responsibility within their inner realm. After all, a soul is always the first responder to a troubled mind, heart, and body. Seizing our rightful position as the foremost responder within our inner realm is vital for each world maker. Just as the Unknowable One besieged and wooed our soul as our Maker, so we must do likewise to our mind, heart, and body. Also, our inner realm will only recognize us as their rightful sovereign if we intend to serve them in fulfilling their greatest desire, making their own unique world for God's world of unique worlds.

Since our inner realm is an integral aspect of creation, responding holistically to our mind, heart, and body is the testing ground Mother Nature uses to identify who is ready for greater responsibility. If we disrespect, mistreat, or malign our mind, heart, and body, then creation will restrict our material access. However, if we gently speak to, touch, and breathe our uniqueness into our inner realm—while simultaneously existing as a being of dangerous, unassailable authority—then creation will cautiously expand our influence. The more our touch upon creation resonates with the Creator's touch, the more our mother will embrace us as one leading her toward becoming our Father's world of unique worlds.

We respond holistically based on what serves our intentions, our partner's intentions, and our Creator's intentions. Each mental, emotional, and physical response we release through our inner realm is akin to a pebble tossed into creation's anatomical sea. The resulting ripples might appear small, but they travel across the entire universal whole. God designed human flesh to work so intricately with Mother

Nature to empower humanity's world-making efforts. The reason we doubt the power of our responses is that we persist in remaining spiritually separate from Power.

A mature world maker fulfills the orchestrational intentions of humanity, creation, and the Creator as a consequence of fulfilling their own orchestrational intentions. Our ancestors exercised their ability to respond by rejecting the intentions of the Creator, creation, and every other human creator so that they might pursue the desire to be like God. As a result, the first man and woman's response has brought about the spiritual, inner, and material chaos to which we must now respond.

Despite humanity's original misuse of responsibility, God has not removed our ability to respond as the authoritatively endowed rulers, fillers, and subduers of His world. Instead, God responded to mankind's rebellion by entering a human body to reclaim creative control and the ability to respond that it endows. How we now respond to our Creator seizing control of our species will determine whether we rise eternally at His side or fall forever as an unalterable void of infinite emptiness.

Presently, our ability to respond remains fully intact. The instant we seize control of and start consciously exercising our responsibility, it will become clear that we are still the original, rightful, and foremost authorities within God's world. The Creator affirmed this truth by taking a human mind, heart, and body for Himself. Therefore, as resurrected spiritual beings we do likewise each day by entering our material humanity so that we might respond to the enemy, to humanity, to creation, and even to the Creator in a way that makes it clear that we are the maker of our world. God wants authoritative warriors, wizards, and wills walking at His side so that each might be a member of His race of unique world makers enabling all to work together toward ensuring the survival, comfort, and orchestration of every world—and every world maker—within His world of unique worlds.

The Seven Uniques

Creation	Outcome	Time	Name
		(Starting Now)	
1. The Unique Body			
2. The Unique Skill			
3. The Unique Enterprise			
4. The Unique Family			
5. The Unique Team			
6. The Unique Position			
7. The Unique Legacy			
		(Ending at 100+)	

www.ingramcontent.com/pod-product-compliance
Lightning Source LLC
Chambersburg PA
CBHW071527040426
42452CB00008B/914